MESSY
VICTORIES

Messy Victories is a work of nonfiction. The authors alone take responsibility for the content of this book. They have tried to recreate events, locales, and conversations from their memories of them. Some names and identifying details have been changed.

Published by The Kolette Hall Company
Syracuse, Utah
www.kolettehall.com

ISBN-13: 978-1-7364854-0-8

Cover design by Christina Marcano
Cover and publicity photos by Tori Hillyard
All other photos by Kolette Hall

Printed in the United States of America
First Printing: February 2021

KOLETTE & JASON HALL

MESSY VICTORIES

A Story of Allowing Grief,
Pursuing Joy, and
Rolling Forward

kolettehall.com

PEOPLE LOVE
MESSY VICTORIES
HERE'S WHY... ● ● ●

I first met Jason over the phone shortly after the tragic accident that led to him becoming a quadriplegic. His determination and optimistic outlook genuinely inspired me. Despite the limitations of his body, Jason was truly a champion. Jason and Kolette navigated life as a team with a winning strategy that you will find right here in Messy Victories. Jason and Kolette's message is a guide for everyone looking to positively and courageously impact their own lives and the world around them--no matter their circumstances.
—DANNY AINGE, PRESIDENT OF BASKETBALL OPERATIONS, BOSTON CELTICS

In this powerful MUST-READ book, you will laugh, you will cry, and you will see how victories are won. You will learn how to look for miracles in your life, apply meaningful principles even when times are tough, and know that you can do whatever it takes.
—KRIS BARNEY, AUTHOR OF *LEADERSHIP FROM THE INSIDE OUT—ARE YOU THE LEADER YOU WOULD FOLLOW?*

Grab a box of tissues and a pen and paper to take note of the Hall attributes that you will want to incorporate in your own life. *Messy Victories* is a must read for all who desire a road map to living their best life.
—BECKY MACKINTOSH, AUTHOR OF *LOVE BOLDLY*

Rarely do we encounter individuals with the innate and adapted abilities to spark personal transformation. Yet the Halls, including young Coleman, seize courage amidst chaos and turn tough situations into building blocks for growth.

—JODI ORGILL BROWN, AUTHOR OF *THE SUN STILL SHINES*

A poignant, heartfelt tale of triumph over tragedy will touch you as this special family shares their hearts and makes their way into yours. Using a firm foundation of faith and gratitude, they reveal how to find blessings in adversity and overcome life's challenges through perseverance, humor, and hope.

—USA TODAY BESTSELLING AUTHOR RACHEL J. GOOD

Opening *Messy Victories* is like sitting down with a close friend. Utilizing [Kolette's] gift for words and the years of stories Jason accumulated, this collection demonstrates how two people took the hand life dealt them and chose to find joy.

—KRISTEN SMITH DAYLEY, AUTHOR OF *FOR ALL THE SAINTS*

Jason and Kolette's book captures the hard won wisdom and enlightenment gained from well-lived lives of adversity and service.

—BRAD BARTON, WORLD RECORD-BREAKING ATHLETE

●●● DEDICATION

For our son, the One and Only

Coleman Jason Hall.

Hey Jason: The dream. It just happened.

HALL FAMILY CHEER

Who are we?

We are the Halls!

Who are we?

We are the Halls!

Who are we?

We are the Halls!

The mighty, mighty Halls.

We are strong, we will conquer,

We stand for the right!

We're full of faith and power,

We will fight, fight, fight!

'Cause we are the Halls,

The mighty, mighty Halls!

THE ORDER
OF EVENTS ●●●

July 13, 1986	Jason breaks his neck at age 15
June 26, 1992	Kolette and Jason get married
1992/1993	Kolette and Jason graduate from Brigham Young University
1992-1997	Jason works as a financial planner for Mutual of New York
1993-1998	Kolette works as an elementary school teacher
November 21, 1997	Jason has a car accident, and he spends the next 13 months in the hospital

December 20, 1998	Kolette and Jason move to Connecticut to rehabilitate near his parents
2002	Kolette starts scrapbook company with her brother
August 2003	Kolette and Jason move back to Utah
January 27, 2009	Coleman is born
May 7, 2010	Kolette is diagnosed with gallstone pancreatitis
April 26, 2019	Avengers Wreck— While driving to a movie, Kolette and Jason are in a car accident
May 24, 2019	Jason passes away

CHAPTER 1
THINGS GET MESSY

Heartbroken.

We took this amazing picture two days ago at Coleman's Decathlon. As of 6:38 am this morning (Friday, May 24), Jason was gone.

Eight hours earlier, he was headed to the ER in an ambulance because he was struggling to breathe. The struggle came on suddenly and has never happened before.
I had our medical aide stay the night with Coleman then followed to the hospital in my car.

They couldn't get his oxygen levels to go any higher than 50.
Finding a strong pulse was a touch-and-go experience as they sent him up to ICU. The incredibly diligent nurses and doctor did all they could—suctioning for what they were hoping would be fluid on and around his lungs.
But it didn't happen. They got nothing.

His low oxygen levels baffled the doctor. He still tried everything.
At 5:10 am, Jason went into cardiac arrest.
The room filled with staff taking turns with compressions, epinephrine, meds, IVs, and anything else the pulmonary doctor called out to do.

Time ticked by. He only had 15-20 minutes before brain function would be affected. His heart started beating at 12 minutes.
15 minutes later he was in cardiac arrest again.
The doctor said that when he first came to the ICU he had no response in his eyes—a sign of injury to the brain.

Jason would not want this. I knew it. His mind is sharp, and it's one of his greatest assets for overcoming the limitations of his body.
I asked them to keep him alive till his parents arrived about seven minutes later.

Then we told the doctor it was enough.
They took him off the machines and called his time of death 6:12 am.

At 6:13, his heart started beating, and his pulse was strong. They were still breathing for him from the bag, and his oxygen was terrifyingly low.
What is this??? Even with all the epinephrine they had pumped into him, they were surprised to see Jason do what he does best—fight harder. Because giving up was never his option.

I laughed and said, "Typical Jason. Let's let him have his moment."
We waited for the heart beats to stop. It took many minutes. With each beat I felt him call out a message to our son. "Coleman. Coleman. I love you. You can do this." Then they stopped.
At 6:38 am.
The man who ALWAYS came back...was gone.

But he is now free. Free from that neck brace. Free from that wheelchair. Free from the constant pain. Free from struggles of a body that doesn't give back.
He can run. He can stand 6'3" tall. He is strong. He is mighty.
Finally.

JASON

When I was fifteen, one of my favorite things to do was ski. Whether the skiing was on the snow or the water, I couldn't get enough of it. You can imagine my excitement when my parents planned a family vacation to Lake Powell for a glorious week of water skiing. Lake Powell is a huge body of water covering 247 square miles and straddling the Utah-Arizona border. The water is so warm, it's like water skiing in your bathtub.

Before the trip, I went to the garage, grabbed my water ski, waxed it up, started sleeping with it. That was November. July finally rolled around, and we loaded our skis in the boat and headed down to Lake Powell.

We put our boat in the water at noon on a Saturday, and by noon on Sunday I was lying on the beach fighting for my life. That morning I had dived into shallow water and broken my neck. In an instant, the trajectory of my life snapped.

They only let one family member ride in the life-flight helicopter with me. My dad jumped in, and they flew me to Grand Junction, Colorado, where I endured the emergency room alone because they wouldn't let my dad in there with me. They poked my foot with a small, sharp instrument and asked if I could feel anything. My worry grew. I could see the doctor at my feet but couldn't feel anything. I saw him poke at my ankle and up my shin. Nothing. He went up my leg and my torso. My fear was palpable with each touch of the instrument. "Feel it! Please! Feel something!" I silently screamed.

My gaze never left that instrument. I saw it come up my chest to just below my arms. "I felt that!" I yelled, making sure that everyone knew I had no intention of completely failing this test. The first poke I felt was four inches from my shoulders. The fear of what that might mean overwhelmed me.

They put me in a CAT scan machine, a big white tube where they took images of my body. I lay there all alone, trying to tamp down the fear and panic. At fifteen years old, all I could think was, "Who will be my friend? Who will want to hang out with a guy in a wheelchair? Who will want to go to a dance with a guy in a wheelchair? Who will want to eat lunch with a guy in a wheelchair?"

The doctor delivered the bad news. "Jason, you've broken your neck. You'll never walk again."

I come from a family of positive thinkers—glass still full even when there are only a few drops left, so I remember laughing within myself, "You're the happy doctor, right? Mr. Positive Attitude!" I joked about it, but the fear was still real. I would never walk again.

They finally let my dad into the room. He was the one who had taught me about that full glass. Dad put his arms around me. We cried together. I know that if he had been given the chance, my dad, my hero, would have traded places with me in an instant. He would have given up anything that he had, *all* that he had, to take this suffering from me. But that's not how hard things work. Incredibly loving and capable people can walk by our side, help us up the rocky struggle of our mountains, make sure our backpack has the tools we need to succeed. But they are still our mountains to climb, and I was standing at the bottom of mine.

After a few weeks, they transferred me from the hospital in Grand Junction to the University of Utah Hospital in Salt Lake City. I spent three months there. I had a neck fusion at the C5-C6 vertebrae and a tracheotomy. I wore a halo brace. I was in traction and a rotating bed to relieve pressure. My mother stayed with me, coming to the hospital every day to sit by my side as her other children, my sister and three brothers, went home to Boise, Idaho. Aunts and uncles, neighbors and friends cared for my siblings. People pitched in when Mom couldn't be in two places at once.

I had no use of my hands or legs, partial use of my arms. I did three months of rehab. I learned to breathe again, learned to sit again, and learned to live in a wheelchair. When I was leaving the hospital, one of the therapists stopped me. She wanted to tell me what to expect in my new life, wanted to prepare me. I'm sure she meant well. I'm sure she just wanted to manage my expectations.

She said that I probably wouldn't graduate with my high school class.
I probably wouldn't ever leave home.
I probably wouldn't attend college.
I probably wouldn't get a job that would pay better than Social Security.
I probably wouldn't get married unless it was to somebody older and substantially more desperate than I was.
She actually said all of these things.

But my parents taught me to dream big and chase those dreams by doing what it takes to make them become reality—even if the chasing was done sitting down with four wheels beneath me.

I graduated with my high school class. I left Boise and attended Brigham Young University, the nation's largest private university, where I was elected student body president. I got a job selling life insurance and was among the top six percent of salespeople in the industry. I met and married the love of my life, Kolette Coleman, who was three months younger than I was. And far from desperate.

Because Kolette could have married anyone she wanted to.

KOLETTE

Jason was in a wheelchair.

We served in student government together. At that time, I knew who he was, but I didn't really know him. I heard him speak at a leadership event at BYU. The room was crowded, and I slipped into the back. As I stood against the wall, he told a short little story about a girl at BYU who broke up with him. People break up all the time. It's a natural part of college life. But in that moment, during an 11:00 a.m. leadership meeting, something stirred in my mind.

"Would I be willing to date someone in a wheelchair?"

It sounds a little crazy, but I *had* to know the answer.
I had to know what I would do if a guy in a wheelchair ever asked me out.
I don't mean that I had to know if I could date Jason.
That wasn't it at all. It really had nothing to do with him.
He was just this guy in student government I barely knew.

The question changed the longer I thought about it. "Could I *marry* someone in a wheelchair?"
Someone. Anyone.
A person in a wheelchair.
Could I do it?

I thought about this question constantly. I could barely sleep because I couldn't get it off my mind. I thought about it when I went out with friends. I walked up the hill to class wondering what I would do. I studied at my favorite spot in the library, working to keep the question at bay. I rode my bike to the copy center for work, asking with each push of the pedals, "What would I do? What would I do?" I prayed to know the answer. It was only a hypothetical question, but it felt so important.

After two weeks of struggle, I started to feel a sense of settling. It wasn't instant, and it wasn't loud. It just started to feel true.

Yes.
I could do it.
I could marry someone in a wheelchair.
I felt assured and peaceful—that familiar peace that comes from knowing a truth for yourself.

Confident in having settled it, I tucked that bit of knowledge to the back of my mind and went on my way, dating different guys and loving college life.

Eight months later, Jason asked me out on a casual date with friends. As student body officers, we visited all the locations of the school dance just for fun. But that "just for fun" date turned into meeting on campus for lunch, going to football games together, sharing a table in the library as we studied.

I learned a little about what it means to be a quadriplegic.
I took stuff out of his backpack for him.
I set up his food so he could take his own bites.
I arranged his papers and handed him his specialty pens.
I pulled on the legrest of his chair when he got stuck in a crack on uneven sidewalk.
I picked up things that he dropped.
I unlocked the door for him.
I opened the door for him.
I pushed the elevator button that might be out of reach.
I saw all of the places he couldn't go because there was no ramp.
I came along as he figured out a way around.

Within a couple of months, we were dating steadily.

Jason was easy to fall in love with.
He was hardworking and positive and funny.
I liked that he was smart and outgoing.

He was the student body president at BYU. Everyone knew him. Even twenty-seven years later, people still stopped us in restaurants or on the street and said, "You were at BYU with me!"

He was fun and always up for going to a dance or a one-dollar movie at the campus theater. He held themed parties in his apartment where we watched *Monty Python and the Holy Grail* or a Hulk Hogan wrestling match.

I liked that he wanted to serve others. He gave twenty hours a week to plan school activities. He was a leader. People followed him to do crazy things like a full-production university-wide forum in the Marriott Center, complete with original musical numbers, skits, and a video describing life at BYU.

You couldn't help but love the things he loved because of his infectious passion. While we dated, I became obsessed with Captain Jean-Luc Picard and *Star Trek: The Next Generation* because he was into it. It was fun being obsessed with the same thing as Jason.

I liked that he had faith and hope and was fiercely loyal to his family.

Jason was in a wheelchair, but he accomplished more than lots of the guys on campus. I liked that.

As we started talking about getting married, people I was close to—well-meaning people, like Jason's therapist at the hospital— tossed questions at me that got me doubting myself.

What if you can't have children?
What if you have to take care of him?
What if you can't do all the things "normal people" do?
What if he doesn't live very long?

I hadn't worried about those things. I had already gotten my answer. I already knew I could do it. But my thoughts about all of those questions undermined my confidence, and I kind of freaked out about it anyway. So I broke up with him right before the Christmas break. I thought, "Maybe I should be worried. Maybe they're right!"

When Jason gave me a ride to my brother's house on his way to catch his flight at the airport, I wanted to take it back. I got out of his van and started up the path. I could feel a physical pressure to turn around and tell him I was wrong. I didn't want to break up after all. But I held my ground and didn't look over my shoulder as I walked to my brother's door.

That night I pulled out a cassette tape with a song our friend had written about Jason. About his diving accident. About how he overcame hard things. I popped it into my stereo and listened. Then pushed rewind and played it again. And again. And again.

The next day, I called him.
It only took me twenty-four hours to remember what I already knew.
I knew I could marry a person in a wheelchair, and I knew I wanted to marry Jason.
Jason was the love of my life.
My friend. The one who made me happy. The one who loved me back.
Yes, I totally wanted to do this.

Those *what-ifs* that well-meaning friends brought up were definitely possible in our life together. But if they happened, they would become part of our story, just like everything else.
We knew that there were always going to be *what-ifs*.
The hard stuff. The challenges.
The things you can predict and the things that punch you in the face because you didn't see them coming.

Everyone knew Jason's disability. He lived almost thirty-three years in a wheelchair. They all saw our hardships and hospital stays and barriers and obstacles. But the longer we lived, the more we understood that everyone has something.
Everyone has a struggle to overcome.
A heartbreak to heal.
A tragedy to bear.
A loss to feel deeply.
A chance to persevere.
We tried not to compare our pain with anyone else's. Everyone has to do the tough stuff.
This book is our story.
We started writing it together.
Side by side.
Planning and laughing and arguing about the best stories to tell.
Remembering and thinking about what we have learned in life.
Deciding the purpose. Focusing in on the message.
And then Jason died.

The man who always came back, who always overcame the adversity, didn't this time.
His fight wasn't enough to conquer.
His hope in the future didn't fix it.
His willingness to persevere didn't matter.

And the ultimate on my list of *what-ifs* has happened.
"What if he doesn't live very long?" they asked me twenty-seven years ago, wanting to warn me, to prepare me, to help me make a wise decision about choosing the guy in the wheelchair.
What if?
I'm living out that question and learning the answer every day.
But I know one thing already.
The journey was well worth the *what-ifs*.

When Jason died without warning, I was shocked and heartbroken.
I truly couldn't believe that my partner—the one I had stumbled

along with, struggled with, made mistakes with, kept moving forward with, overcome with—was no longer doing life with me.

I imagine him in Heaven. I know he is there without the challenges of a quadriplegic body to weigh him down, making friends and watching over Coleman and me. My broken heart feels a bit of peace, even joy, as I talk with him in that "after death" way that puts him nearby.

I exclaim, "Look at what we just did, Jas! Can you believe it?"
You will see Jason here.
The volumes of stories he has told for the last thirty years, stories from his presentations and videos and writings, stories that shaped and taught him.

You'll see me here.
My take on it all.
Things I've tried that worked.
Stuff that failed but I learned from.
My lessons and thoughts from life with a quadriplegic.
My social media posts after he died.
The journey I'm still on.

The way we lived our life together prepared me for the moment Jason would leave. Jason and I learned resiliency. We learned perseverance. We learned gratitude and grief and goodness. We learned to look for miracles. We learned that even when it all seems terrible, everything is still going to be okay.

I have an image of us in my mind, making our way to the winner's podium of life, battered and bruised, crawling.
Shoulders weighed down with fatigue from the challenges that had our names on them.
Sitting there, worn out from the everyday battles, breathing heavily with the exertion of doing the best we could during our twenty-seven years of marriage.

Then we look at each other. Smile. And laugh while we give each other a high five. "We did it!"

It wasn't always pretty, and it was never perfect.
It was messy. It was blundering.
It was make-it-up-as-we-go and fly-by-the-seat-of-our-pants.
We didn't always get it right.
But we stuck with it. We learned things.
We worked hard. We never gave up.
We got better. We overcame.
We loved. We laughed.
We doubted and feared right alongside choosing happiness.
Sometimes we got it right.

Those messy victories.
Sometimes we actually won.

"Look at what we just did, Jas!" I say, laughing.
And I feel his response surround me. "Yep, we did it."

Struggle. Pain. Adversity. Faith. Hope. Gratitude. Grit. Grief.
It's all here in this book.
We're here.
Because no matter how far apart Jason and I are, we're still in this together.

FACEBOOK POST – JANUARY 11, 2020 (DAY 232)

Have you ever been NOT excited for the new year?
Not looking forward to a fresh start?
Not anticipating tackling a goal to become a better you?
Not ready to move forward?

Jason has been here every year for the last five decades.
Now I'm facing a sequence of four numbers that won't have him
in them.
2020.
A new year. A new decade.
I can't help but drag my feet. Look back with longing.
Wanting to hang on to 2019. The last year that Jason was with us.
I don't want to step into January and leave him behind.

A scripture says, "And he knoweth their faith, for in his name could
they remove mountains."

Grief is a mountain.
I'm sure that many of you would agree with this.
Loss. Empty places. Heartache.
It's a mountain.

Faith can move that mountain.
I totally believe that our mountains can be moved or made easier
or at the very least, become bearable burdens.

But what if grief is not a mountain that I want to remove just yet?
What if I don't want to move on from it?
What if I don't want it flattened or conquered or overcome?
What if I just want to feel it?
To feel him.
To keep him with us.

I've decided to carry my mountain into 2020.

The tears. The feelings. The thoughts. The sudden waves of
loss that take my breath away. The joy of remembering. The
tender moments of comfort from angels both on this earth and
from a higher place. And the stories. My favorite thing of all.
The stories.

I'm inviting Jason to hold my hand and walk into this new year with me.
In whatever way he is allowed.
He would have liked 2020! I'm sure of it!

Jason, I refuse to leave you back in 2019.
You're coming with me.
I am not leaving you behind.

CHAPTER 2
EVERYBODY HAS CHORES

FACEBOOK POST – AUGUST 3, 2019 (DAY 71)

Coleman and I always shared a closet and bathroom.
I know, that sounds totally weird.

Jason always had an aide who came in the morning to help with his care, get him dressed, and get him out of bed.
The aide came back at night to repeat the process in reverse order.

I never wanted to get ready in the same room where the aide was doing his work, so I always used a different closet and bathroom in the house.
Makes sense, right?

When we moved into this house, we were doing IVF, and I didn't know if I would become pregnant.

So I used the guest room closet.
The room that became Coleman's.

He was just a baby. Babies are tiny and their clothes are tiny, so sharing with him was easy.
I knew I would move to a different closet and bathroom someday when he got a little older, then I never got around to it.

Now he's ten.
And pretty much I'm lazy.
I never moved my clothes, and we still share a bathroom.

When Jason died, I decided to take over the closet and bathroom in our bedroom.

I mean, come on, even I could see that sharing with Coleman when we have 13 closets and 4 bathrooms in the house seems kinda ridiculous.

But I didn't want to pack up Jason.
Put him away.
Move on.
I'm not ready for him to leave that closet.

I decided to share.
After 27 years of marriage, I'm sharing a closet with my husband.

My shirts touching his shirts.
My shelves near his shelves.
Perfume sitting next to cologne.
Our closet.

I cleaned out a little bit—just the stuff that he didn't really care about—and left the stuff I love.
Moved it over, condensed a bit, stacked it higher.

I don't need to access it every day.
I just want to see it, be near it, be with it.

The ties he paid to have shortened because he sat down all the time and didn't like them too long.

The tons of baseball caps—do you REALLY have to get a new one every year for your favorite teams???
Now I'm glad he did that.
The pocket squares—a more recent staple in his wardrobe—lined up on a shelf so he could pick the perfect one to go with his tie.

The button-down shirts on dry cleaner hangers, heavy starch.

The polos arranged by color.
For every two shirts there's one with a BYU logo...just sayin'.

The suit coats—my favorite because he was determined to look sharp even though he was in a wheelchair.

His sweaters and sweatshirts. Those perfectly folded piles still live in the closet.

His three pairs of shoes in excellent condition—sneakers, dress shoes, and casual—no walking means they never wore out (handicap perk).

His cuff links.
The ones that look like a Superman comic.
The ones made from Yankee stadium seats.
The ones from his grandpa.
The ones from his dad.

His clothes.
My memories.
Our closet.

Of all the places, I feel him most in that closet.
I like sharing with him. At last..

JASON

A few days after I broke my neck at Lake Powell, my dad walked into my hospital room with his hand behind his back. I had just undergone surgery to fuse my vertebrae, and I was in a halo brace.

"Jason, I just want you to know that in our family everyone still has chores."

I couldn't speak because of my tracheotomy, but my eyes darted in his direction like, "Okay, I don't think I'm going to mow the lawn or empty the dishwasher or make my bed anytime soon. I'm not sure what you're driving at, Dad."

That's when he showed me the 5x7 index cards.

He called these my "chore cards," and every day I had to look at them and do what was written on the cards.

My first chore was to visualize—visualize things I could see myself doing, including walking. I imagined myself doing all kinds of great things: driving our friend's Porsche, walking on the beach in the Bahamas. Believing that it could happen. Believing that God works miracles.

My daily goals were written on another card. I had to pray every day and read scriptures about faith. I had to listen to something motivational every day like Earl Nightingale's *The Strangest Secret* or one of Zig Ziglar's cassette tapes. I had to listen to positive music. I had to watch or listen to something funny each day. I watched a lot of Don Knotts and Tim Conway movies like *Private Eyes* or *The Apple Dumpling Gang* on VHS.

Dad listed my strengths on two more cards, what I was good at and how that would help me overcome this new life challenge. My job was to read those strengths three times a day.

JASON . . . YOUR STRENGTHS

1. RIGHTEOUS ... THE LORD WILL BLESS YOU
2. OBEDIENT ... BLESSING PREDICATED ON THIS.
3. LOVE FOR OTHERS.. CHRIST SAID LOVE ONE ANOTHER
4. LEADERSHIP ... INFLUENCE OTHERS FOR GOOD
5. CONFIDENCE ... WILLINGNESS TO TRY
6. FAITH ... FAITH TO BE HEALED
7. DETERMINATION... TRY, TRY, TRY, NEVER GIVE UP
8. GOAL SETTER ... THIS WILL MAKE THE DIFFERENCE
9. POSITIVE ... AS A MAN THINKETH...I THINK I CAN
10. HAPPY ... BE OF GOOD CHEER
11. SMART ... YOU WILL LEARN QUICKLY
12. CREATIVE ... YOU WILL FIND A WAY OR MAKE ONE.

13. SENSE OF HUMOR ... A GREAT PART OF GOOD HEALTH
14. SELF RELIANT ... DO ALL YOU CAN ON YOUR OWN THE LORD WILL MAKE UP THE DIFFERENCE.
15. MUSICAL .... LISTEN TO POWERFUL, MOTIVATING MUSIC, LISTEN TO SPIRITUAL MUSIC, MUSIC THAT ATTRACTS THE HOLY GHOST.

16. SPIRITUALITY ... THIS IS THE GREATEST TALENT AND GIFT. PRAY, PONDER, MEDITATE LISTEN TO THE SPIRIT, THE HOLY GHOST, WILL COMFORT, TEACH, INSPIRE AND DIRECT YOU IN ALL YOU WILL DO.

Chore cards.
Something to do every single day.

Those cards gave me a purpose. They gave me direction. They gave me something to focus on instead of my hard situation. They gave me hope and encouragement, like maybe my dad thought I still had something to contribute to the family, that

GOAL: Set a goal for each week

VISUALIZE: See yourself walking
Think about it
Beleive you will
Tell your subconscious mind
Your most dominate thought

Think about driving Bob's Porsche
Think about walking on the beach in the Bahamas.
Think about tracking in the mission field
Think about the power of God to make it happen... He loves you.

1. Book of Mormon ... 1/2 hour each day
   (Prophet asked each to do this)

2. Motivation tape ... 1 each day

3. Read strengths .. 3 times each day

4. Music. ... 1 hour each day

5. Faith scriptures .. read each day

6. Pray ... Morning, noon, night
   Prayer in your heart

7. Humor ... watch or listen each day

my life was still worth living, that I was valuable even though I couldn't move my body. I had to do chores. I mattered. Those cards were my assurance that my dad would never give up on me. And with that, I knew I wasn't going to give up on myself.

KOLETTE

At 5:10 am, I closed the automatic garage door and hopped into the car with my neighbors. It was January, pitch black and freezing cold. We headed to the local gym, huddled together in the minivan with water bottles in hand. If we carpooled together, our chances of actually showing up for a workout increased approximately eighty-three percent.

Thirty minutes later, as I glanced up at the gym clock to see how many more seconds I had to go in my sixty-second plank, I looked at the people around me.

"I wish I had her skinny arms. I bet they totally fit in every sleeve she has with room to spare," I thought, with a dose of dejection to chase down the self-criticism.

"Wow, I'll never have the discipline to look like her. How much time does she spend here anyway?" My elbows physically felt the added burden of my thoughts.

"At least I don't have as far to go as he does. Good luck with that weight, dude," I thought, trying to elevate myself by shoving someone else down.

My eyes were twelve inches off the ground as I scanned my fellow early-morning exercisers, comparing myself to everyone around me.

Everyone.

I live within a fifteen-pound body weight range.
When I'm at the bottom of the weight range, my confidence is high.
I've got this!
I eat a mega-salad every day.

I go for high protein, low fat chicken breasts and love it.
I can totally deny the Little Debbies calling to me from the pantry.
I look dang good!

When I'm at the top of the weight range, I feel like a failure from all the negative things I tell myself.
Why can't I keep the weight off?
I have no self-control.
I'll never be able to do this.
I might as well eat those Little Debbies in the pantry.
I hate what I see in the mirror.

During my hour at the gym, my mind never stopped the critical labeling and categorizing of each person who came into my line of vision. But ultimately, the most impactful labels I was dishing out were the ones I was giving myself.

I don't measure up.
They are better than I am.
I should keep noticing my failings.
I should keep noticing theirs.
Competition is how it's done.
I'm not enough.
Why try?
I'll never be enough.

By the time I finished my exercise routine that day, I had come to an uncomfortable realization. I was officially in the habit of feeding myself negative self-talk on an almost continuous basis, and I was believing all that stuff I told myself.

I could feel the weight of my own negativity pushing on me, pressing into me, darkening my spirit. I couldn't look at my body in the mirror because I was so afraid that what I saw would be so much less than what I wanted, evidence of not measuring up to some standard I had established for myself but was failing to reach, proof of my falling short and knowing I was "less than" whatever I had determined was good.

You would think that because I lived with someone whose body hardly works at all, I would be less critical of my own body. But I had some serious body-image issues. The snare called "Negative Self-Talk" had me wrapped tightly in its unrelenting cords.

Wait. How could this be? I'm the sunny, cheerful gal whom everyone can count on to say the happy thing, give the smile, see the bright side, overcome the tough stuff.

My blood type is B+, for heaven sake! Positivity is literally in my DNA!

At that moment lurking inside my brain, I felt the tentacles of a menace that had spread into every nook and cranny of my personal peace, my inner joy. It was stealing my sense of who I really am with every critical thought and seemingly innocent comparison.

When Jason's dad wrote out those chore cards for Jason in the hospital, he included two cards called "Your Strengths."
A handwritten list.
Sixteen of Jason's qualities and how they would help him overcome the seemingly insurmountable challenge he faced.

One of Jason's daily chores was to read his list of strengths three times each day. Jason had a tracheotomy, a hole in his throat where a tube was inserted to allow him to breathe. He was in traction. He couldn't move his arms or his legs or his head. Jason's mom spent hours at his bedside holding up the "Strengths" cards so Jason could read them the required three times daily.

Positive self-talk.
Sure. Just be positive. That's all.

As I left the gym that frosty morning, I knew this simple practice was the first step in shifting my disparaging self-image, but the habit of comparing had become ingrained in my head without my even knowing it.
I was mired in negativity of my own mind's making.
And I wasn't sure how to change it.

It was a few weeks after my "Sixty-second Plank Epiphany" that an idea came.

Jason often taught about his hospital chore cards in his motivational speaking assignments. He asked me to create a PowerPoint slide that showed the cards. I needed to tidy them up so people could see them clearly.

I opened the images of the cards on my computer.
I read them over, looking for ways to see the words more easily.
I created the slide, reading the list of words over and over.
And a simple but trajectory-changing question came to my mind:

"Do you have to be fifteen years old and lying in a hospital bed for someone to tell you your strengths?"

Pause.
"Well," I thought to myself, "do you?"

No.
I don't have to be fifteen years old.
I don't have to be in a hospital.
I don't have to a teenager facing the struggle of my life to fight back.
To draw my sword in the war of negativity and begin the battle against discouragement and self-deprecation.

I don't have to experience a tragic accident to discover my strengths.

I can do it now.
As a mom.
Forty-four years old.
With a career and a child and a husband.
With my mind caught in the habitual trap of comparing and labels and not measuring up.
I can do something about it now.

So, I began.
I pulled out a notebook and started creating a list of my strengths.

Number one: Teacher. I have a Master's degree in Education, and I'm pretty confident in my ability to teach. Teacher, number one on the list: Done.

Number two: Also easy. I was once a card-carrying member of the National Association of Professional Organizers. I am organized.

I wrote *teacher* and *organized* then, in Stephen Hall's chore card fashion, I added a short phrase about how each talent helps me and others live better, what I give to the world because of this strength.

But it got harder pretty fast.
Although I like hearing compliments from others, I felt the inner cringe of discomfort as I thought about writing more strengths.

Doubt.
Maybe I was kind of good at some things but are they really considered strengths? Am I really strong in them? Am I really that good at them? Good enough to write them down in my notebook?

Doubt began to swirl in my mind as I wondered, really wondered, if I had anything else to say about myself.

I felt insecure.
Maybe I should just abandon this project.
Maybe I should just be confident in the knowledge that I am super-organized and an awesome teacher and leave it at that. That's pretty good, right? Maybe I should just be happy with Strength One and Strength Two.

"Or maybe you could get some help," that voice in the back of my mind whispered.
My shoulders sagged just a little because I knew that voice was right. I could get some help.

On my birthday, I received cards and texts. Along with birthday wishes, many of my friends and family also wrote nice things about me.

I pulled the good stuff from these messages, the things that people said they admired about me. I used those as my strengths. I wrote them down on my list and added a brief sentence about how each strength helped me or others.

I asked trusted sources: Jason, my sister, my closest friends. "What would you say are my strengths?" They told me. I chose to believe them and wrote everything down.

My list slowly grew.
And my focus slowly shifted.
The thoughts in my head, those lethal judgments that destroy the divine truth about myself, were being challenged.
Holes formed in my previously formed self-image.
Tiny holes called "teacher" and "organized," hard-working" and "creative."

"Mother" and "problem-solver," "purposeful" and "says the right thing."
My strengths. Holes.
Holes that nibbled at the negativity.
Holes that took on the shape of love.

I began to feel greater compassion.
Compassion for myself. Compassion for others.
Gentleness for my own imperfect but exceptional journey.
A little more confident. A little less comparing.
A little more courage. A little less criticism.
More love.

Sometimes the scale reads more than I want it to. Sometimes my arms aren't as skinny as I want them to be. Sometimes I struggle with food. Sometimes I go for the easy choice instead of the healthy one. Sometimes I do all of that.
But sometimes I don't.
And no matter what I struggle with, there is always something that I am good at. Something I have mastered. Something I do that helps others. Something I give that fills a need perfectly.

My strengths. I'm not perfect, but I'm always awesome at something. And so was Jason.

JASON

I had been in the first grade only a few days when I found out about a worldwide elementary school health hazard. In some schools this hazard was called "Cooties." At my school, it was called "Molly Germs."

Molly was a little girl at my school who somehow got pegged as the carrier of this dread disease. All us kids had to be extremely careful when we got to school in the morning because the first person Molly touched got infected with "Molly Germs." That child would have Molly's germs until he touched someone else and passed off the dreaded disease to the next unlucky kid.

Molly reacted the way most of us would. She became angry and frustrated and, I'm sure, very hurt.

After a year or so, Molly moved away. As I grew older, I began to understand how I must have made this little girl feel. I wasn't the one who came up with the game, but I didn't stop it either. I simply went along with the rest of the kids, spreading "Molly Germs," never thinking how it would make Molly feel.

When I was about eleven, I met a man who was an amazing example of treating people with kindness, much better than we had treated Molly. His name was Joe. Joe and his wife were a young couple in our neighborhood.

I loved Joe. He was my scout leader and my buddy. My friends and I often rode our bikes to his house, and he always had a story to entertain us. Sometimes he took us to get ice cream at the local drive-thru. Joe was a hero.

One day, Joe asked if I would do him a favor. Of course I would! His daughter from a previous marriage was coming into town, and he asked if I'd be willing to show her around.

When you're eleven years old, showing someone around town means taking them to the arcade and down to the gas station for a soda. But this was Joe asking. I was determined to do my best to show his daughter a good time, even if that meant fronting her some quarters to play PacMan. He told me how grateful he was for my help. Things had been difficult for his daughter since the divorce. He hoped a great experience in Boise would make a big impact on her life.

The day before his daughter came to town, Joe stopped by to make sure I was still willing to help out. I told him it was all I could think about because I was so excited. "I'm so glad," he said. "I know you and Molly will have a great time."

My heart stopped as I put two and two together. Molly from the first grade and Joe had the same last name. Molly of "Molly Germs" was Joe's daughter. My face flushed deep red. I was completely ashamed of the way I had treated my friend's daughter. Luckily, when Molly arrived, she had no memory of me. I was relieved I was so forgettable. I worked the entire weekend to make up for the things I regretted doing as a first grader.

I learned a great lesson that day, a lesson that had a different meaning only a few years later.

I was in choir my sophomore year in high school when our group embarked on the annual choir trip from Boise to Salt Lake City, Utah. I hadn't been home from the hospital very long and didn't have my power wheelchair or accessible van. My friends pushed me from place to place in Salt Lake City.

In Salt Lake City, my friend Krishel was pushing my wheelchair across the street when a man in a power wheelchair passed us going the opposite direction. Krishel leaned down and whispered, "Can you imagine what it would be like to be in a wheelchair?" I chuckled and told her that I could probably imagine it. She realized what she had said, and we had a good laugh about it.

For a second, Krishel forgot I was in a wheelchair.

She saw me. Jason. She didn't see the wheelchair or the quadriplegic. She didn't see the "Cooties" or the "Molly Germs." She simply saw her friend.

I'll never forget the impact that had on me.

KOLETTE

I took my first art class in junior high.
One project required us to choose a picture from a magazine,
cut it in half, mount half to art paper, and draw the missing half
to match the original.

I was into it.
I sketched the shapes of the image. I shaded in expertly.
Darkness, light, blending, I had it all, and I was super proud of
my finished product.

I got a "C" on the project.
All semester I couldn't seem to create what my teacher was
looking for.
I got a "C" in the class.
I was devastated. I loved art. But obviously I didn't have what it took.
I told myself I wasn't an artist.

A couple of years later, my mother asked me to do some lettering
for her.
My job was to write out a poem my mom wanted to use and
make it look pretty.
I wasn't sure if I could do it.
"I can't do it as well as you can," Mom said. "I need your skill."

I took the responsibility very seriously. I practiced and prepared
the final version.
I thought it was pretty good for a sixteen-year-old.

My mom thought I had skill. I started to believe her.
The first file folder I ever created was labeled, "Lettering."
I began watching for interesting ways to write words.
I collected copies of menus, programs, and advertisements.
I sketched examples of signs and billboards and quotes.
I saved them in my file folder.

I sat at the kitchen counter and practiced. And practiced. I filled my room with inspirational, handwritten quotes. I got to the point where I could recreate any lettering I saw.

Later, my brother Kent and I started a scrapbook company. We sold stickers and paper and other scrapbooking supplies. I usually used other graphic designers to create the vision of what was in my head because I didn't have the computer skills to do it myself.

When we launched our company, the technique of tearing and crinkling paper and then layering it to create backgrounds and other scrapbooking elements was becoming popular. I tore paper, crinkled it, layered it, then we took pictures of my creations and printed them to sell.

At our first tradeshow, we were a hit. Retailers bought our whole line of products.
At our second tradeshow, Colorbök, a large crafting company, offered to buy our company and put our products in Walmart.
We didn't want to sell the company, but we offered to design a line of products specifically for them.
"Okay," they said. "Let's do it."
We were stunned. No one in the industry had ever had such an agreement before.

I got to work right away on the Walmart presentation, but I didn't have computer skills.
I layered flower-shaped paper on backgrounds and glued them down. I tore strips and inked edges. I printed on vellum then used brads and grommets to attach it to more layers. I crafted backgrounds and embellishments all by hand.
Total DIY.
It felt so inadequate for a big presentation.
So basic.
But it was all I knew how to do.

Jason and I were moving to Utah the same week the product samples were due to Colorbök. I worked feverishly to pack the apartment, fill the moving van, and finish the presentation.

The morning we moved out of the apartment, I finished the presentation and loaded my stuff in the van. Our drive from Connecticut to Utah would take us right past the Colorbök offices in Michigan. I decided to deliver my samples and presentation in person.

The president of the company was there and so was the sales rep who had championed us from the start.
I pulled out my samples and described how the products went together.
The president left the room.
I stopped talking, wondering if I had failed already.
He came back with a couple of people.
The sales rep left the room.
She came back with more people.
They all started talking, moving my samples back and forth, touching them, inspecting them. Discussing. Planning. Brainstorming. Strategizing.
I heard the words "layer" and "embellished." My eyes darted around the room as I tried to take in what was happening.

"Are you saying you can make these products layered like I made them? You don't have to just take a photo and print them?" I asked.

"That's exactly what we are saying."

Creating my samples, I felt inadequate and insecure and unsure. No one in our industry had created complete, layered, three-dimensional papers and stickers before. I didn't even know that was possible.
But the Colorbök team knew it was totally possible.

That meeting was the beginning of a new path for me.
We were some of the first to create layered embellishments for crafting.
I had a top-selling kit on QVC with Colorbök.
We won an industry award for being the first to collaborate as two separate companies on the same product brand.
I learned from amazing designers and sales people who taught me how to think bigger.
I taught classes and workshops all over the country because of Colorbök.
I went back to school to learn graphic design because of Colorbök.
I launched my career as a licensed designer because of Colorbök.
I have designed numerous products for the craft industry because of Colorbök.
The Colorbök team knew what was possible. Now I know it too.

I almost believed my junior high art teacher.
I almost thought I was only worth a "C."
I almost believed I wasn't an artist.

Thank goodness I listened to my mom instead.

JASON

Grandma Hall had a tradition for birthdays or other special days. She would gather us around the kitchen table and encourage each of us to share something we liked about the person having the birthday.

My dad loves this tradition, so it has proudly been carried on with the next generation. It doesn't matter if you are a family member or a guest at the table, you are required to say something nice about the special person. One year for Mother's Day, we brought our friends Keith and Rushell with us to a family dinner. We warned them they might have to participate in our family tradition. They didn't believe us. After dinner, my dad announced it was time to tell Mom what we loved about her. Our friends thought they were off the hook since they had just met Mom an hour earlier.

Nope.

Everyone said something nice about Mom. It happened just like we told them.

At first, it feels a little uncomfortable telling someone why you love them. Out loud. It also feels a little uncomfortable hearing what people have to say. But this is a practice thing. If you do it enough, you get better at actually saying nice things about people, and you get better at listening to what is said about you. Maybe you even start to believe it.

When Kolette taught school, she carried on Grandma Hall's tradition with her fourth grade class. The birthday girl or boy would sit at the front of the room on the special teacher stool. That was lucky enough. To make it even better, the child had full control of Kolette's stick jar, the jar full of craft sticks with each student's name on them.

The birthday girl or boy pulled a stick, read the name on the stick, and asked that person, "Why do you like me?" Each child responded.

Stick after stick, compliment after compliment until the birthday girl or boy eventually came to their own stick in the jar. The student would say, "I like myself because..." and tell everyone a really good reason.

I like that fourth grade self. I want to be the one who pulls his stick and calls out, "I like myself and here's why!" The one who is confident and cares for others and tells everyone why they're awesome, too. I want to be that guy.

KOLETTE

I like Jason for a lot of reasons, but one of them is that he was an excellent snow and water skier before he broke his neck. He could completely jump across the entire wake on a water ski and never missed the chance to land a flip on the frozen terrain.

Jason did some snow skiing after he broke his neck. With his sit-ski and a #dominatethemountain kind of instructor named Tom, they did stuff up there that no one with Jason's level of movement should have been able to do.

I, on the other hand, never learned to ski as a kid.
Although I've taken lesson after lesson, I have never really gotten the hang of skiing. Mostly it just hurts my knees, and I look forward to relaxing outside the lodge with my feet up, watching for Coleman to make his way to the lift for his next run. #dominatethehotchocolate

It was because of both of our experiences that Jason and I wanted Coleman to be a skilled and confident skier at a young age.
We live thirty-five minutes from the ski resort.
We enrolled him in lessons at age four.
By the time he was eight, he was pretty good on that mountain.

I took Coleman out of school one day to ski with cousins. In an effort to be the "I guess I'll do it because I don't want to be a lame mom" kind of mom, I decided to give skiing another go. We went down the bunny hill so I could get my bearings and were headed up the lift for the second run when Coleman said, "Mom, you are doing a really great job. Something you might want to think about is putting your skis together more like French fries instead of like pizza."

"Coleman, you are exactly right," I replied gravely, fighting the laugh that was threatening to escape. "I will continue to think about it every single second as I painstakingly make my way down this hill."

Not recognizing my attempt at a joke for what it was, he nodded. "We're going to get off the lift soon. Put your tips up, scoot to the edge, and put your poles in your right hand. You can do it."

All day long he was patient with his slow, unadventurous mom, waiting for me at various stopping points, taking the "straight down through the trees" route with his cousins while I just took my time, back and forth, back and forth across the hill.

On the way home, I realized something.
"Coleman, you are patient, and you explain things in simple ways so I can understand. I never knew it, but you are a really good teacher."

And the question I had asked myself a couple months earlier came full force to my mind: "Do you have to be fifteen years old and lying in a hospital bed for someone to tell you your strengths?"

No.
You can be eight.
Life can be awesome.
And you can still have someone tell you how great you are.

I took the white 4x6 notecards and a Sharpie marker that were in my drawer in the kitchen and started writing.

One strength per card.
A few sentences about how that strength would help Coleman in life.
Next card.
We attached them to his closet door.
When we think of another strength, I make a card and stick it on.

38

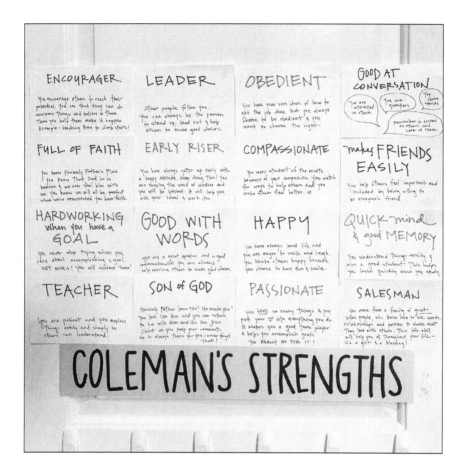

For his third grade Economics Fair, Coleman was assigned to take twenty-four items to school, price them, and sell them to his classmates. "What two strengths on your door will help you the most today during your Economics Fair?" I asked.

He picked "good salesman" and "works hard when you have a goal."

"I totally see those helping you. You're going to do great today!" I said.

And he believed me.
Because his closet said so.

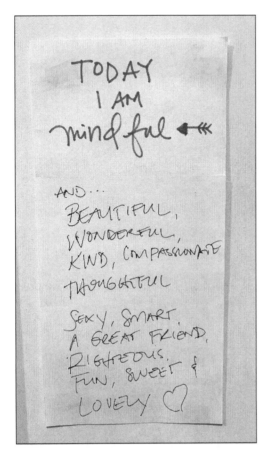

About six months before Jason died, I wrote myself a note. A goal on a 4x6 card. Something I was working on. It said, "Today I am mindful."

One day, my note had changed. Two more cards had been added to mine. On them were sixteen words in Jason's handwriting.

I put that list in our closet, you know, the one we now share, so I can see it every day.

And I believe it.
Because my closet says so.

FACEBOOK POST – FEBRUARY 11, 2020 (DAY 263)

Performances start this Friday for Coleman's play.
"Joseph and the Amazing Technicolor Dreamcoat."
Jason and I saw it years ago in Toronto – with THE Donny Osmond.
It's a family fave, for sure.

This youth theater group runs on hard work, laughter, and parent volunteers.
For the last few years, I have had the same volunteer spot.
Stage Left.
With my friend Debbi.

She is in charge, and I am happy to do what she says.
We manage the props table.
We help with quick costume changes, zipping dresses and pulling off accessories just in time for the next scene.

There's action. There's downtime. Coleman is around. I'm with my friend.
Volunteering for Stage Left is fun.

I got an email this year.
"Stage Right," it said.
The regular Stage Right coordinator needed help because her mother was sick. Someone who could be in charge in case she had to leave.
They were asking if I would do it.

I froze.
My heart stopped.
I even started to panic just a little.
All I could see were the words "be in charge."

The old Kolette would have said, "Sure! I can totally do that."

But I'm still not the old me. I'm the new me. The one who shies away from volunteering. The one who lets others sign up first. The one who panics just a little when asked to be in charge.

I took a deep breath and called our producer.
"Beth," I said, "I can't do it.
I'm forgetful and instructions are hard for me right now, and I know it's not that big of a job but this feels super stressful."

She supported me 100%, and another mom stepped up to conquer Stage Right.

I know. Bummer, right?
The old me might want this story to end differently too.

Kolette rising to the challenge, busting through her panic, and singing in a triumphant Broadway voice, "Yes! I will overcome! I will do Stage Right!"

But this is still the new me.
The one who knows that a victorious ending can look like a lot of things.

It can look like showing up.
It can look like smiling.
It can look like being kind to a rambunctious pre-teen actor.
It can look like an encouraging word to a nervous dancer.
It can look like tweaking a mic cord or fixing a hair clip.

And it can totally look like that safe space called, "Help Debbi with Stage Left."

Stage Right is handled.
Everything is taken care of.
It's ok if I'm not quite ready to be in charge yet. I can still be victorious.

Come see the show.
I'll be on Stage Left.

CHAPTER 3
WE TRY LEFTY MODE

FACEBOOK POST – FEBRUARY 26, 2020 (DAY 278)

I often walk to the cemetery.

The local cemetery is tiny.
It's within walking distance of our house.
I walked around it with my family members, holding a map of the available plots.

I looked at the names on the neighboring headstones.
Elsie. Eunice. That was it. Those were his people. I just knew it.
I chose the plot between them.
I knew that Jason had already introduced himself and made friends.

My neighbor Kristy lost her little boy Luke in a drowning accident years ago.
He is buried at this same cemetery.
Kristy and her husband have ten-year-old twin girls who are friends with Coleman.
They often visit Luke as a family.

The week after Jason died, I asked Kristy if she and the girls would take us to the cemetery.
To learn the ropes. To see how it's done. To experience it with the masters.

The girls told Coleman to bring his scooter.
We started the mile walk as the kids scootered ahead.
The girls taught Coleman to climb and hide in the tree by the bench.
They taught Coleman to jump up high on top of the towers while Mom takes a picture of you.
We traveled up the small hill to the cemetery.
They taught Coleman to run to Luke's grave to check it out.
They taught him to race to the statue of the angel.
They darted from grave to grave, fixing the flowers that had fallen over and inspecting the names etched in stone.

Kristy told me stories of the cemetery, the history of it.
Her son Tate planted the trees around the perimeter for his Eagle Scout project.
She taught me about cleaning days twice a year and a special luminary ceremony at Christmastime.

We showed them where Jason would be buried. Right by Elsie and Eunice.
Then we made our way home.

Kristy and the girls taught us how to do the cemetery. It was a place of love and hope and remembering. It was even a place to play.

We invited Jason's parents to come visit the cemetery a few days later.
Then we did the same thing for my family.
This time Coleman was in charge.
He showed them the tree, the bench, the water towers.
He showed them Luke's grave and the angel statue.
The cousins propped up flowers that had fallen over as they ran among the rows of headstones.
They met Elsie and Eunice and learned where Jason would be buried.
"Don't rush the funeral."
Two people told me this after Jason died.
I took their advice.

It gave me time to think and to remember and to feel Jason near me.

By the time the funeral rolled around, we had been to the cemetery half a dozen times.
We knew this place. We knew the people there.
Kristy and the girls taught us how to do the cemetery.

I'm glad we didn't rush the funeral.

JASON

My dad had an annoying love of Sunday drives, family togetherness type Sunday drives. When I was a kid, Dad's nostalgic Sunday drives were some of my least favorite hours of family time.

It was the 70s, and we had one of those big green station wagons with wood paneling. Every Sunday, Dad would load all the kids into that car, and we'd go reminiscing.

We'd drive by the schools he and Mom had attended, the houses they'd grown up in, the first house they bought, the parks where they used to play. The stop we dreaded most was the lamp post. "Kids, that's where I used to kiss your mother."

Gag. When you're eight, you know that your dad has to kiss your mom, but you really don't want to know any more than that. For my parents, Sunday driving was sheer bliss. For us kids, it was utter misery. No matter how far we went, it couldn't be over soon enough.

Every summer, my dad loaded the same kids in the same car and took us on a vacation. It didn't matter how far we had to go or how long it took, we were enthusiastic the entire ride. We sang the *Hall Family Song* or some version of *99 Bottles of Milk on the Wall.* We laughed and talked. We played the ABC Game until our vision went blurry. It didn't matter how far we were going. It didn't matter if we left at 4:00 in the morning or 10:00 at night, whether we had four hours or sixteen hours to go.

Same kids, same car. What was different?

The destination.

We knew where we were going. We were excited to get there. We had purpose. And that changed everything.

KOLETTE

When Jason and I were student body officers at BYU, we learned how to ask the right questions when organizing activities and programs. It was called "Planning with a Purpose," and we practiced it relentlessly.

The first step was to identify what we valued. What we really cared about and what was important to us.

Next we asked the "Golden Question."
Some people might think that if you're planning an activity, the most obvious question to ask is, "What are we going to do?" and that would make a lot of sense.

But when planning the dance or the pep rally or the service project, our mentors taught us to change the question.

"What do we want to have happen?"

This question is kind of magical really. It's only slightly different in wording but tremendously different in purpose.
Instead of thinking about the activities we were going to sponsor,

we began by thinking about the outcome we wanted to achieve.
What feeling were we trying to create?
What relationships were we trying to strengthen?
What problem were we trying to solve?

This slight change in the question shifted our mindset and shifted our planning.
It helped us focus on the end result instead of the event itself.

Once we had established what we wanted the outcome to be, the next question became, "What is the best way to make that happen?"
Plans were made, events were scheduled, and decorations were designed based on the Golden Question, always focusing on what we wanted to have happen.

The Golden Question gave every activity purpose.
The Golden Question changed everything.

The Golden Question doesn't just apply to college activities.
Jason and I found it worked for everything.

Some people think peer pressure ends when you grow up and leave school.
It doesn't. It just takes other forms.
"Peer Pressure" is nothing compared to "Parent Pressure."

"If you want Coleman to be healthy, you have to puree fresh vegetables and make your own baby food. You should follow these people on Instagram. Everything's totally organic and made from scratch."
"If you want Coleman to play high school sports, you have to commit to a competition team by the time he's eight years old. Why is he still playing rec ball? You might want to step it up."
"If you want Coleman to get into an excellent college, he must know all of the multiplication tables and be able to read on a

junior high level by the time he finishes first grade. Here are some flash cards to help."

I want to be a great parent. I want to do it right! But when Jason and I tried to follow the advice of all those well-meaning parents, we found ourselves running in circles, trying to keep up with an expectation that we weren't even sure we believed in.

One day Jason and I looked at each other and wondered.
Were we good parents?
Was the parent pressure getting to us?
Maybe it was.
And then we realized that in the quest to be "good" parents, we had lost sight of what we truly believed was important. We had looked for advice on everything, getting opinions from neighbors and family members and Instagram.

In all of that searching for information and answers, we had forgotten to ask our never-fail question.

"What do we want to have happen?"

We stopped, for just a minute, and asked it.
What do we really want to have happen with this little human who has been entrusted to our care? When he has graduated from high school and is ready to take the next step, what do we want for him?

The answers came surprisingly easy.

We wanted to raise a child who is confident and kind, who works hard and loves life.
We wanted to raise a child who serves others willingly and makes good choices.
We wanted to raise a child who is full of faith and hope.
We wanted to raise a child who can cope with emotions, even in the middle of hard things.

Once we understood what we wanted, we sat back and breathed a sigh of relief. Our purpose became clearer and so did our ability to decide how we were going to show up as parents.

We wanted Coleman to have the chance to be full of faith, so we went to church and tried to have daily prayer.
Each week, we read scriptures for a few minutes together as a family.
And when we faced hard things, we talked about how we could still choose to live with faith.

We wanted Coleman to experience serving others, so we looked for ways that we could serve together.
We put away neighbors' garbage cans on trash day.
We encouraged Coleman to do something each day at school to help someone.
We showed up to help our neighbor lay sod. We showed up to take a meal to a family.
We announced service loudly in our house, "Our family is now going to go serve!" so that Coleman knew exactly what we were doing and didn't miss a message cloaked in subtlety.

We wanted him to know how to cope with his feelings, even when it was difficult.
We talked about how sometimes things don't work out like we want them to.
We tried to model what it looked like to allow our emotions and choose positive ones if we could.
We talked about how to look for what was good when we were discouraged or hurt or heartbroken.

None of the things that we did were really that dramatic. They often took very little time and effort. Most of it was what we were already trying to do as a family.

Something had changed though.

We became more deliberate.

The things we really cared about began to shift to a higher place on our "To Do" list.

The things that didn't align with our answers to the Golden Question faded in importance. They became easier to set aside.

Coleman still went to lacrosse practice and theater rehearsal. We still tried to eat healthy, and we wanted him to be a good reader. He was still active and busy and involved. But we started carving out a little bit of time to accomplish the things that would get us the results we actually wanted.

Parent pressure was edged out by parent peace.

We could focus more on what we felt was right instead of being swayed by the opinions of others.

We made choices that fit our family, more confident choices.

We knew where we were headed, and we were more excited to get there.

Our purpose, and the peace that comes with it, became more clear.

JASON

When I first broke my neck, I was in rehab for a few months. In rehabilitating from just about any accident, you are required to be up and moving as soon as possible. Because of this, the patients in my rehabilitation unit were required to take our meals in a community room on the rehab floor.

Each day, all the patients with physical and mental disabilities headed to the day room to have our meals. I have stayed in a number of hospitals all over the country, and the common thread among all of them is that the food is bad. But as bad as the food was in our day room, the conversation and comradery made up for it.

Luckily for us, we were each given a pass once a week to skip the day room meal and go to the hospital cafeteria instead. To the average person, eating in the cafeteria may not seem all that exciting, but to someone who ate hospital food every meal, it was the highlight of the week. There is nothing better than a grilled cheese sandwich from a hospital cafeteria. Since we were only allowed one pass per week, we saved our trip to the cafeteria for a day when the food in the day room was especially bad.

On one particular day at the end of the week, all of us had used our cafeteria passes. We ate buffet style, and when the food arrived, the server loaded it into the buffet line. This is one of the few days I remember the exact words that came out of the server's mouth when she told us what was on the menu. With an excited look on her face, which I now believe was just an act, she said, "For dinner you are going to get a delicacy: cooked bananas wrapped in ham dipped in cheese sauce."

There was a long pause as we waited for her to crack a smile and tell us she was joking. Somewhere in the silence of that pause, she turned and left the room. Somebody pulled the foil from the serving pan, and there it was just like she had warned us, cooked bananas wrapped in ham dipped in cheese sauce. I have no idea where this dish is a delicacy, but I do know that I have little interest in traveling there.

We were stuck. We had already used our cafeteria passes and were starving after physical therapy, but we refused to eat cheesy ham bananas. We made a plan. As a group, we formed a wheelchair gang, rolled to the nurses' station, and asked if just this one time, they would overlook the rule of one pass per week.

With a pack of patients before them, the nurses took pity on us and relented. We got our passes and had the happiest elevator ride I have ever taken. I am quite certain our chances of getting passes that night would have decreased substantially if we had gone one by one to the nurses and asked. It would have been easy for the nurses to insist we only had one pass per week and to encourage us to deal with the bad food.

But together we were strong. As a group, we could not be beaten. We knew what we wanted, made a plan to get there, and accomplished it together. Being one in purpose was powerful, powerful enough to get everyone a grilled cheese sandwich.

Sometimes even when we know our purpose, our method needs a little adjustment.

When we moved into our current home, we didn't have any children, but we wanted our house to be a place where the nieces and nephews wanted to hang out. The cool place. Because we were the cool aunt and uncle.

Kolette bought two video games, *Dance, Dance Revolution* and *Rock Band*. I thought she was crazy because she spent way too much money on two games I couldn't even play. We set up *Rock Band*. Kolette figured out the guitar. It wasn't long before she was totally shredding it. Then she moved on to the drums. Since I don't have any movement in my hands, the guitar wasn't an option for me. I can't hold drumsticks so the drums were also out. I did the only thing I could. I sang. Lead singer of *Rock Band*. I crushed "Enter Sandman" and "Should I Stay or Should I Go" and the rest of the set list.

For two hours.

You can only dominate "Wanted Dead or Alive" so long before you're ready for the next challenge. Kolette, the problem solver, had an idea. She took some Ace bandages, tucked a drumstick in each of my hands, and wrapped the heck out of both of them. I kind of lost circulation, but those drumsticks were anchored to my hands. We spent the next two hours jamming out to

"Learn to Fly" and other favorites with me on the drums. My score was dismal. Kolette was fierce on that guitar, and I couldn't keep up. I had to get better at that thing. I decided to look at the tutorial section of the game. There was something magical called "Lefty Mode."

Because I am right-handed, I was playing the drums right-handed, but because of the way I sit in my chair, I was unable to reach all four drums and kept missing beats and points. When Kolette switched me to "Lefty Mode," I could play with my strong side. Suddenly, with this little bit of information, my success doubled. "Lefty Mode" transformed my whole experience.

That's the way it is when we struggle to accomplish something. At times we need to take a step back, reassess our strengths, and make a small adjustment. That small adjustment might make all the difference in purposefully moving toward the result we're looking for.

After I broke my neck, I had to get a new license to drive. I had a license before the accident because in Idaho, kids can drive at age fourteen. When I came home from the hospital, I had to get relicensed using the hand controls that operated my van. I soon found I had a fairly significant problem. My arm wasn't strong enough to turn the steering wheel to the left. I only had enough strength to make right turns. I don't know exactly why, but the man who gave me my driver's test passed me, even though I couldn't make a left-hand turn.

I took that license and ran, or rather rolled, quickly out of there.

I went everywhere making only right turns. Starting each journey out of my driveway, I drove in right hand circles until I eventually ended up where I needed to be. This happened every morning on my way to school. Unfortunately, when I got to school, I couldn't make a left-hand turn into the parking lot, so I had to park on the street. If there was no parking on the street, I went around and around the block until somebody moved or I ran out of gas.

This extra disability didn't deter me from saying yes when a girl asked me to the next school formal dance. I was really excited. This was my first girl-ask-guy dance, and I would be able to pick up my date and drive her to the dance myself.

I decided it wouldn't be very manly to tell my date I couldn't make left-hand turns, so I kept it to myself. I simply mapped out a right-hand route to the restaurant and then the dance. On the night of the dance, Suzie and I sat in front and another couple sat in the back. On our way to the restaurant, Suzie completely ruined my plan. "You need to get into the left lane." I corrected her. I'd mapped out the route, and the restaurant was on the road straight ahead of us. "We changed the location of dinner," she said. "It's a big surprise."

No kidding, it was a surprise.

I don't know what I was thinking, but I truly did not want to embarrass myself. "Maybe," I reasoned, "my arm is strong enough today to make the turn." I pulled into the left lane and tried to turn the steering wheel left with all my might. I knew I was in trouble when the laws of physics kicked in. There is a force exerted on your body when you drive a car around a turn. You automatically tilt in the opposite direction. As I made my left-hand turn, my body leaned to the right and kept leaning. Normally, my seatbelt would have caught me, but the tuxedo I wore was either too tight or my chest was too large, and that night, I wasn't wearing my seatbelt. As that force pulled me to the right, I fell into my date's lap, and we had instant runaway van.

My van crossed the lanes of traffic going the opposite direction and rolled into a field next to the freeway. We were on a collision course with a huge green power pole when my date had the presence of mind to shove me back into sitting position and yank the steering wheel so we wouldn't hit the pole. I pushed on the brake, and we stopped in the middle of the field, our hearts pounding wildly. I turned to my date. "I can't make left-hand turns."

"You think?" she said.

Thankfully, my friends situated me in my chair, and we got the van back on the correct road. After a delicious meal and a great time at the dance, the thought of botched left-hand turns was a distant memory, but I was smart enough to glean a moral lesson from the experience: Always, always choose the right.

My purpose was to get us all to the dance. I created a plan and tried to carry it out. I mapped it out, taking into consideration my limitations. Sometimes things go wrong, even with our best efforts and planning. Sometimes we choose left when the best answer is to choose right. Or maybe we're playing from the right when really, we're at our best in "Lefty Mode." But it's okay. Identifying, remembering, and focusing on what we want to have happen helps us get to our destination, even if we make a few wrong turns along the way.

The first day I started selling life insurance at Mutual of New York, I went into the office to learn side-by-side from my highly successful manager, Chuck. My dad had been a thriving insurance salesman with the same company, and I grew up believing in the product. I wanted to be just like my dad and create something great in the life insurance business.

Chuck told me to bring in a list of one hundred names, people who knew me, leads I could call who might be interested in buying life insurance. I was ready.

Chuck forgot it was my first day.

He already had a full day of appointments. Apologizing, he cleared off his desk and invited me to move into his spot. He placed the phone in front of me, handed me his calendar, and said, "Take out your list of one hundred people, and start calling."

He left me alone with my list, the phone, and an almost debilitating fear. I had no idea how to sell insurance, no idea how to convince people to meet with me. Sitting there all by myself, my first-day excitement and confidence evaporated. In an instant, I wasn't even sure I wanted to do this anymore.

I stared at the phone as the sweat began to form on my brow and my heart rate increased. Then a photo on Chuck's desk caught my eye. It was a picture of Chuck's family in front of their beautiful home. That picture represented everything I wanted in my life, every reason I had pursued this career in the first place. That picture was my purpose. I simply wanted to be able to take care of my family.

I looked at that phone again and thought, "If I want to get to what's in that picture, I have to go through this phone." I took a deep breath, picked up the receiver, and punched in the number of the first person on my list.

As I learned that day and many hard days afterward, true purpose inspires devoted action.

FACEBOOK POST – AUGUST 19, 2019 (DAY 87)

I did something today.

The year we were married, Jason was the student body president of BYU.

The next four years he ranked among the top six percent of salespeople in the life insurance industry and qualified for the Million Dollar Round Table.

Year five, his front tire blew on his handicap-accessible van, and he spent thirteen months in the hospital.

With almost ten years of surgeries and recovery, he was never able to go back to selling insurance.

Many agents work years to make it to Million Dollar Round Table. Jason did it in only two months his first year in the business.

His dad was an insurance guy.
Jason inherited his massive sales skills from him (and Coleman got them too!).

This family believes in life insurance.
His dad took out a policy on Jason before he broke his neck. Those premiums, when he was young and in perfect health, were tiny compared to the ones we paid after.
We paid premiums when we could barely pay rent.
We even said yes to a policy when Jason was rated Table 16 – just one step above denial.
We got Coleman's first policy when he was born, complete with as many riders as we could get to secure future insurability.

This family believes in life insurance.

About eight months before Jason died, he and his brother Clint (another agent in the family), went through our policies to make sure everything was in order.

T's were crossed, and I's were dotted.

When Jason died, the sadness was crushing.
The shock still lingers.

The emptiness will stay forever.

But worry over our financial security was a fleeting thought.

We believed in the system.
And the system worked.
I didn't worry about paying the mortgage or rushing back to work.
I didn't worry about finding policies or rounding up files.
We had done that already.
Clint had everything he needed to help me.
I didn't have to worry.

It's an interesting feeling to deposit a check that feels like a gift from the person you love.
The person you miss.
The person who is still providing even though he is gone.
The person protecting you.

I did that today.
Thanks, Jas, for loving life insurance.

CHAPTER 4
I PULL SEVEN WEEDS

FACEBOOK POST – JUNE 22, 2019 (DAY 30)

What have I been doing this week?
I have a list.
It's a special list.
It's called a "Realistic List."
Ever had one of those?

I add all the things to it that come to mind that need to get done.
If it's not on the list, it's lost in space.

These are actual things that need to get done.
No "maybe-I-shoulds" make it to the Realistic List.
This is not the time for non-vital tasks, right?

And it's kinda freeing to allow yourself to only do the things that matter most. I wonder how long I can keep this state of mind?

I choose one thing on my Realistic List to do each day. If I do more than that, I'm a ROCK STAR!

So I do TWO things on the list...because who doesn't want to be a rock star?

I often ask for help. Like when I went to visit the cemetery and Jason's flowers were crumpled and dry.

I just couldn't throw them away by myself. It hurt my heart to think of doing it alone.
So, I listened to my heart...

I called my friend Patty, picked her up, and drove the five minutes back to Jason. She found a dumpster, and we tossed them in.

Together was easy.

JASON

I'd been home from the hospital for about six months when one night at the dinner table my dad asked what we wanted to do for our family activity that week. Once we gave our opinion of what we wanted to do, we were allowed to eat dessert. We were all excited for dessert, and it was an especially good day for me because my dad asked the oldest kid first. I weighed in on what activity I wanted to do, got my dessert, and dug in. Next, my sister gave her opinion and also started eating her dessert. The next two brothers followed. By the time my dad got to six-year-old Nathan, the rest of us were so focused on our ice cream headaches that we almost missed Nathan's suggestion.

"Nate, what do you want to do for the family activity?"

Nate turned to Dad, so serious, so sure. "I want to teach Jason how to walk." We all pulled our faces from our ice cream bowls and tuned into the conversation.

"Well, Nate, what if he falls?" Mom asked.

"We'll stand him up and do it again." Nate had faith I would walk again, and he was ready to act on that faith.

When Kolette and I built our first house in Lehi, Utah, we had barely graduated from college and both had new jobs. Needless to say, we were on a tight budget. One day, a man came to our neighborhood selling pine trees out of his truck. The price was right so I bought two, and we planted them in the corner of our front yard.

Three summers later, one tree was thriving. The other tree was decidedly not. The needles began to dry out and turn brown. I consulted with people at the plant nursery to find a remedy. I fed it nutritious concoctions, added fertilizers, gave it more water, and dug a trench. I also bought a small decorative rock ornament to place beneath the tree with the word "faith" etched into it. I felt that if I just believed, the tree would survive.

Weeks passed. More trenches. More fertilizer. More faith. But the tree deteriorated. I was determined not to give up. One morning, we went out to work on the tree and saw something new. A rock had been placed in front of my "faith" rock. "Reality," it said. We got offended for about half a second then started to laugh. That rock was right. I needed a serious reality check. The tree was not going to make it, and no matter how much faith we had, reality was still going to intrude.

We've got to have faith. We have to act on that faith. It's what gives us courage and allows us to believe that anything is possible. Faith keeps us from despair and discouragement. Faith gives us hope, and hope is what keeps Kolette and me from giving up. But we have to be okay with reality too.

In a funny way, embracing reality also creates hope. It's highly unlikely that I will walk in this lifetime. Like my little brother Nate, we have faith that I will walk someday. But we also have faith that we can do everything that comes with being a quadriplegic. We have faith that our reality is not just an unfortunate mistake but actually an indispensable part of our life journey.

KOLETTE

Jason and I have faith.
But our faith has to find a home inside our reality.
Believing that good things are possible and available and all around us, even when we know that our swirling storm will not subside – that's faith.
Hanging on, moving forward, and not giving up even though our circumstance or obstacle or adversity does not and will not change – that's faith.
We have faith that living our reality is how we will grow into exactly who we are meant to become.

Faith draws breath from the future and exists within our reality. It has to, actually. Otherwise we would have no hope.

There are six kids in my family.
Our names all start with K: Kara, Kyle, Kory, Kolette, Kamron, Kent.

We grew up in a three-bedroom, two-bathroom house.
My four brothers slept in one room, my sister and I shared another. We all battled for time in the bathroom.

After dinner, my mom would take a quick inventory of the table and countertops. "Everyone take care of thirteen (or seven or twenty) things," she would say. That meant for each of us to choose thirteen things to put away, including rinsing and placing our own dishes and silverware in the dishwasher.

The rush to grab the salt and pepper shakers was lightning fast. They were small, and they counted for two items. A serving spoon was one. The entire casserole dish was one—don't get caught having to deal with that! Fifteen minutes later the kitchen was clean. No one complained about being stuck with KP duty, and only minor fights broke out while grabbing for the same item.

There was something about being able to focus on less that made cleaning the kitchen easier. No one had to do everything, including my mom.

I'm pretty organized. I get that from her.

I used to be a member of NAPO, the National Association of Professional Organizers. You probably didn't even know there was such an organization for us fastidious types.
I am good at making charts and systems.
I'm fantastic at setting goals, writing them down in a cool way, and creating a plan for conquering all areas of my life. I'm also pretty good at accomplishing lots of my goals.
But as I've gotten older, I've learned some things about me and goals—our relationship, I mean.
It's complicated.

Maybe you're like me:
I get super motivated to plan my goals. I love writing them down, using different colored pens and a variety of fonts and making them look cool. I even love starting my goals.

Then I start to feel overwhelmed.
It's hard to keep up with those multi-colored goals.
I wonder if maybe I should give up.
But wait! I have a cool chart and an awesome plan and multi-colored pens.
Come on! I'll be such an amazing person when I accomplish all these goals.
The motivation still fizzles out.
Along with my goals.

My days of comprehensive, every-area-of-my-life goal setting are over.
I'm not interested in all of them anymore.
My reality is that I really only work on one goal at a time.

Not one goal at a time in each area of my life. Nope.
Just one goal at a time. Period.
One focus.
One choice.
One change.
One thing to try.
One thing to improve.

JASON

I don't remember a time when having a PMA (Positive Mental Attitude) wasn't a regular part of the life skills that my parents taught me. On July 13, 1986 my life changed in an instant. I went from being a completely healthy young man in the best shape of my life to being paralyzed from the chest down with only partial use of my arms and no use of my hands.

The first nights were the most harrowing. My lungs filled with mucus to the point that the doctors could barely see any clear part of my lungs on the X-ray. You didn't have to have a medical degree to understand that my life was in the balance.

All I wanted was to wake up the next morning.

Later, when I began to feel like I was on my way to something better, my dad came to the side of my bed and asked me if I felt like I could deal with life as a quadriplegic. I looked him in the eye and said, "I can do anything for eighty years."

Not long after I came home from the hospital, a man who held an important responsibility in our church came to stay with us. His name was Robert Harbertson. We knew he was important because for months before he came, my mom drilled us on proper table manners. All of a sudden, extra spoons and forks appeared at our place settings. My mother taught us to eat politely and use the proper silverware even when eating Spaghetti-Os. That is quite an accomplishment.

On the day of his arrival, my dad drove to the airport to pick up Brother Harbertson while my four siblings and I sat in our best Sunday dress waiting for them to come. We were—each of us in our own way—thinking how Brother Harbertson might help us. I knew he would have great nuggets of wisdom to share with me and knew he could help me better deal with my disability.

He came into our home—an eruption of happiness and joy—with a smile so wide it almost didn't fit on his face. Brother Harbertson approached me first. "Jason, I'd like to see you pick your nose."
Of all the wisdom I thought he might impart, all the words I would have guessed he might say, asking me to pick my nose had never once entered my mind. But I had learned to respect my elders, so I attempted to pick my nose. There is only one thing more embarrassing than picking your nose in front of someone you hold in high regard, and that is being unable to pick your nose in front of someone you hold in high regard. My arm muscles were too weak to lift my hand to my face.

"That's okay," he said, with a sparkle in his eye. "Next time I see you, I want you to be able to pick your nose." For months after that, I worked hard to pick my nose—almost every day. To be clear, this is something you do alone. This is not a tag team event. Every day I would sit in my room by myself and work to get my hand to my face so I could pick my nose. Almost six months later, I saw Robert Harbertson again. "Jason, I want to see it!" he said.

I will tell you this: If I know anything, I know that there has never been a nose picked with more vigor and excitement than happened that day. I mean, I *really* picked my nose. I wanted there to be no question I had accomplished the task he had assigned me.

In truth, Robert Harbertson cared very little that I could pick my nose. What he did care about was that I had the strength in my arms to wash my face, feed myself, and brush my teeth. He understood that the more physical strength I gained, the more independent I would be. He wanted me to be as strong as possible, even with my physical limitations.

KOLETTE

Deciding that he could do anything for eighty years was just one thing.
Learning how to pick his nose was just one thing.
But that one thing led to the strength and skill to do other things.
Each "one thing" led to more independence.

In 1997, five years after Jason and I were married, Jason was driving his handicap-accessible van down the Interstate on his way to a sales appointment. There was an automatic ramp so he could get into his can, and he drove it using hand controls for the gas and the breaks.

He heard what sounded like a shotgun firing as his front left tire exploded. He fought with the steering wheel as the van careened left, over three lanes of traffic, through the median, and into oncoming traffic. Cars came barreling toward him as he crossed the northbound lanes facing south. His van hit a car ,and a car hit him before he came to a stop on the sloped shoulder of the Interstate.

His vehicle was totaled, and his body was bounced from his wheelchair. He was found hanging half-in and half-out of the passenger window.

I rushed from my fourth grade class to the emergency room. Jason was a mangled mess of broken bones lying on the gurney. His head bled from a wound that would require thirty-five stitches. His legs were twisted awkwardly.

The first thing we checked was Jason's wrist movement.

Being a quadriplegic, he had no use of his legs and hands and partial use of his arms. If he could move his wrists, it meant he hadn't sustained more neurological damage. We sighed with huge relief and gratitude as his wrists moved up and down.
It was painful for him, but they moved.

Jason ended up staying in the hospital and at the care center for thirteen months. It was the hardest thirteen months of our lives.

His list of injuries was extensive, and the complications of being a quadriplegic only compounded the problems and the recovery time.
-*crushed legs*
-*broken hand*
-*smashed teeth*
-*pulverized knee*
-*head wonds*
-*threatened lung capacity*
-*lack of stamina*
-*intense pain*
-*pressure sores on heels from lying down*
-*pressure sore on tailbone from sitting up*
-*weight loss from low activity*
-*weight gain from steroids*

After those thirteen months, Jason was ready to leave the care facility but far from ready to live life.
We needed help.
We rented out our home in Utah and moved to Connecticut to live with Jason's parents.

A transport service took us straight from the care facility to the airport.
We expected to be in Connecticut for six months.
Recovery for a broken and battered quadriplegic did not happen as quickly as we anticipated.

He endured surgery after surgery.
Hospital after hospital.
Six years later, we left Connecticut to return to Utah.
It took Jason a full ten years to recover from that accident.

JASON

Immediately after that car accident, they took off my watch and ring in case my body swelled up. Have you ever had a black eye? It swells. They anticipated my body would be one giant black eye, and they were right. My arms bulged with fluid. I looked like Popeye.

The fluid that builds up in your body after an accident has to go somewhere. After it stops filling your tissue, it travels to your organs. On my second night in the hospital, the fluid built up in my heart and lungs, restricting their function and endangering my life. The fluid built up so dangerously that the doctors told my family if they were going to say goodbye, they needed to do it immediately. They didn't believe I would make it through the night.

Luckily, nobody told me I was on death's door.

By about 3:00 in the afternoon, it felt like an elephant was sitting on my chest. There was so much fluid in my lungs, I couldn't breathe. The only way to relieve the pressure was to put a tube in my nose, thread it down my throat into my lungs, and suction out the accumulating fluid.

Every hour and a half, I asked the respiratory therapist to come to my room to suction out my lungs. As the night wore on, the times between suctions got shorter and shorter. At 3:30 in the morning, they suctioned me again. Before the therapist had made it to the elevator, I told the nurse, "He's got to come back and do it again."

The nurse, knowing what the doctors had told my family, put

her arm around me. "Jason, you don't have to keep doing this."
I looked at her with all the determination and force I could
muster. "If I don't do this, I'm going to die! And I don't want to
die! So bring him back in!"

I was focused on one thing, staying alive, and I didn't care who I
had to inconvenience to do it.

The therapist came back.
And came back.
And came back.
Finally, in the morning, I could breathe a little better.
The time between suctions got longer.

My "one thing" that night: I held onto life with all my might.

KOLETTE

Five years into Jason's recovery from that fateful car accident, I
started a scrapbook company with my brother Kent. I ran it from
Connecticut for a short time until we moved back to Utah. We sold
paper and stickers and crafty embellishments. My responsibilities
included overseeing product design and marketing. Kent was the
money and operations guy. He fulfilled every order to scrapbook
stores around the world, managed our inventory like a champ,
and made sure we didn't spend too much.

Twice a year, we launched a new product line. I hired artists and
designers to help create my vision for what we would bring to
the next trade show. Once the designs were complete, we used a
local commercial printer to print our product.

Since there are many scrapbook companies located in the state
of Utah, everyone was on the same schedule we were, all trying
to get products ready at the same time.
The printing presses ran all night.

Which meant press checks ran all night too.

If we were launching new sticker sheets or paper packs, I had to press check each one.
When it was our turn for printing, whether in the middle of the day or the middle of the night, I went to the printer every few hours to check a new sheet.

The press was loaded with four colors of ink—CMYK. Cyan, magenta, yellow, and black.
The press operator would show me the sticker sheet.
I'd double and triple check the die cut lines to make sure they were in the right place.
I'd double and triple check the text for any typos.
I'd double and triple check the header and title and company information.
And we'd double and triple check the color.

The press operator would pull out his printing loupe, a specialized magnifying glass without a handle. He'd place the loupe on the sample sticker sheet and put his eye close to the lens to see how the color lay on the paper.

Sometimes the color wasn't placed correctly, and the images looked blurry.
Sometimes the color was offset from the die lines.
Looking through the loupe, each of the four inks could be seen as individual dots of color. When magnified, we could tell how each dot related to the others.

To the naked eye, those four inks created a whole and complete image in a rainbow of colors.

One bottle of cyan.
One bottle of magenta.
One bottle of yellow.

One bottle of black.

Point by point, those individual colors came together to make something so much more than what they were on their own.
When Jason learned to pick his nose, it led to being able to comb his hair, lift his fork to his mouth, and eventually drive his accessible van. One thing, leading to one more thing, leading to yet another thing, creating so much more than what they were on their own. That's a heck of a lot of power in just one thing.

Three weeks before Jason died, we were in another car accident. A driver turned on a yellow arrow in front of us as we went through the intersection.
The van was totaled, but we thought we were fine.
We went to the emergency room anyway. They did X-rays on us both. Jason had seven broken vertebrae.
He had been sitting in his chair after the accident, moving his neck and his body just fine, so I definitely didn't expect that diagnosis.

Since the fractures weren't affecting his spinal cord, he stayed one night in the hospital and went home with a neck and chest brace.

My back ached, and as the days passed, the pain worsened.
We both moved slowly for a couple of weeks.
One morning, I walked out to my front porch and looked at our yard. It was spring. Our yard was filled with those post-winter weeds that seem to shoot up overnight.

My back hurt. We had no van, so I had to do all the driving in our rental. We had physical therapy and doctor appointments and end-of-school activities.
I groaned out loud at the thought of bending over to pull those weeds.

I decided to do just one thing.

The flower bed right next to the porch is enclosed, surrounded by the house and sidewalk.
I pulled those weeds.
Counting one, two, three, four, five, six, seven.
Seven weeds.
That's what I pulled.

I walked back into the house, completely satisfied with myself.

Sometimes my reality is nurturing the flowers, laying the mulch, and tackling every unwanted plant out there.
Sometimes my reality is pulling seven weeds.

Being real with myself about what I can and can't do, what I should and shouldn't do, is like releasing a burden of my own making.

I like that girl with the multi-colored pens. I like her charts and plans and long lists of lofty goals.
But I like the realistic, simplified version of her better.
The girl who has faith but acts on that faith in a way that is real for her.
The girl who has hope but knows that unmet hopes don't mean failure.
Using a couple of colors instead of the whole package.
A post-it note stuck to the refrigerator to replace the chart.
A plan and vision that she actually wants to achieve without giving up.
That girl conquers big goals.
She just does it by picking one thing at a time.
That girl is a rock star.

FACEBOOK POST – OCTOBER 26, 2019 (DAY 155)

I bought something at a particular athletic clothing store.
They gave me my purchase in a bag that said, "Hope is not a strategy."

I get what they are saying.
If you want to exercise, just hoping you will exercise is not going to cut it.
If you want to eat healthy, just hoping you'll eat healthy isn't going to make it happen.

But I still have to disagree with my bag.

Coleman and I went to Lagoon, a local amusement park, with some friends.
I had never seen the Sky Coaster.
Coleman and two of our older teenage friends waited in line for over an hour to ride that thing together.
In a standing position, they strap you to a harness.
Then pull you up to a crazy height.
And disconnect.
You free fall.
And start swinging a couple of hundred feet in the air.
What the....?????

This is exactly opposite of what I would choose to do. Heights freak me out.
I could see Coleman biting his lip and shuffling from one foot to the other as they strapped on the harnesses and cracked jokes and waited for the people in front of them to take their turn.
He was freaked out too.

Coleman is two feet shorter than Cody and one foot shorter than Dallin, the two teenagers who volunteered to do this crazy stunt with him.
They put Cody, the big guy, in the middle.
As they swung, Cody got squished by the outside guys.

Coleman swung by and shouted, "Let's gooooo!!!"

When Coleman got off, he said the Sky Coaster was the best moment of his life.

People often asked Jason and me, "How do you do it? How can you be happy within all of your challenges?"

I think our way was probably similar to your way too.

We had hope.

We knew our life had a purpose.
We knew we were meant to have trials and adversity so we could learn things.
We knew we were meant to overcome and endure those same challenges.
We knew they wouldn't last forever.

And we knew that we are meant to feel happiness in the middle of it all. That gave us hope.

We are kind of like those three boys on the Sky Coaster.
One boy represents our grief.
One boy represents our hard things.
But the big guy, the guy in the middle, is hope.
Sharing space with the difficulties that press in on every side.
Standing still, hanging on, anchoring us in the moments of free fall.
Keeping us strong as we swing back and forth from high point to low point.

Hope coexists with our challenges.
Happiness lives right next to our grief.
Joy is possible, even in the middle of hard things.

Hope is the big guy in the middle, and my bag from that athletic store is wrong.

Hope is actually our ultimate strategy.

CHAPTER 5
JASON MAKES A RUN FOR IT

FACEBOOK POST – JULY 8, 2019 (DAY 45)

There is a story in the Bible of a man who gave his servants five, two, or one talent, according to their ability.

The servant who was given five talents doubled his and so did the servant who was given two talents.

The servant who was given one talent buried it. He was afraid of losing it.

The reckoning with their master was joyous for those servants who created more with their talents.
But the one who hid his talent had to give his one puny talent to the guy who had ten.

Not the best choice to bury that talent.

Here's what I think.

Before he came to earth, Jason was probably assigned to the five-talent group. He could do a lot of things really well, so it makes sense he had five talents to work with.

He also knew he could double those talents with persistence, hard work, and some charisma thrown in for good measure.

Total confidence that he could turn the five into ten.

But then the Lord said, "Ok, I can tell that you're going to do a great job with those talents. Let's see what you can do with this," and he handed him one of those vests with weights in them that people use to make their workout harder.

"Just put that on. Carry that around with you, and every so often we'll add a little more weight to it. You can still turn those five talents into ten. I believe in you."

So he did it. Jason put on that vest and committed to carrying whatever weight it held. Confident that he would not give up.

But it was heavy.
Really heavy.

Then the Lord said, "I know it's heavy. Maybe even more than you can bear. So I'm here for you. As a matter of fact, there's a spot for me in that vest to stand right beside you and carry that weight with you. We'll do this together."

And they did.

I like to think that's how Jason's own "Parable of the Talents" went down.

KOLETTE

When I was a kid, going to the lake meant boating and swimming and kayaks. These days, along with all of the normal activities, there are huge bouncy playgrounds anchored in the middle of the lake equipped with trampolines and ladders and slides. They're totally fun, but pulling yourself up onto one of those things takes serious arm strength.

At the Hall family reunion, Coleman easily scrambled up the "Iceberg," an enormous white blow-up mountain with handles placed strategically along the steep sides. He was ready to jump off the top into the water below.

And he wanted me to do it with him.

There was a problem though.
First of all, I would have to pull myself up there.
Second, I would have to jump off.

Heights kind of scare me.

But striving to be the "fun mom," I sometimes put myself in situations that don't feel very comfortable. No way was I wimping out in front of my son.

Pulling myself out of the water using the first set of handles was hard.
I got my footing on the lower handles and muscled my way to the top.

There I was, at the top looking down, my heart beating triple-time.
"What have I done?" I thought.
Coleman waved to me encouragingly from the water below. "Come on, Mom!"
There was no way I was going to get down the same way I had come up. Jumping was the only option.

I thought of Eleanor Roosevelt, who said, "Do one thing every day that scares you."

I closed my eyes.
I breathed deeply.
I repeated Mrs. Roosevelt's quote like a mantra.

And I jumped.

It felt like my heart stopped beating, and my breath caught in my throat for the few seconds it took me to fall the twenty feet to the water.

Then SPLASH! I landed next to my son, the reason I'd jumped in the first place. "Good job, Mom! Let's do it again!"

"You're on your own, buddy. Have fun!" was my reply.

I had no desire to repeat the experience.
But I had done it.
I had jumped even though I didn't want to.

Hard things are exactly that. Hard.
Unfortunately, life is full of hard.

JASON

For months after I broke my neck, I didn't have the arm strength to lift my hands to my head. My mom combed my hair for me every day. One night, I was getting ready for my first formal dance at the high school. I was all dressed up in my tuxedo—white with a lavender cummerbund. You gotta love the 80s.

I had the corsage, we had dinner reservations, I was set for a great night. I turned to my mom and handed her the comb so she could do what she had done every day since my accident. A smile grew on her face. "Jason, how many sixteen-year-old boys are going to have their mom comb their hair tonight?"

"That's ridiculous! Nobody's going to have their mom comb their hair!"

84

She handed me the comb. "That's right. Nobody."

Uh. Thanks a lot, Mom.

I did my best to comb my hair that night. It looked horrible. But I instinctively knew the days of my mom's combing my hair were over. I had to figure it out or be stuck with bad hair for the rest of my life.

KOLETTE

I think a lot about Jason's mom during those years after he broke his neck. Making him comb his own hair took some serious Mom Guts.

It couldn't have been that difficult for her to comb his hair every day.
It probably didn't take that much time, and I'm sure she was a lot faster at it than Jason was.
She could definitely do a better job than he did.
His life was hard enough. Shouldn't she have made that one thing easier for him?

But Sophia knew something.
She knew that Jason had to figure it out.
She knew he wouldn't grow if she always made the way smooth for him.
She knew that even though it was hard, Jason had to learn how to do it himself.

One day when Coleman was about seven years old, he asked to play with a friend. It was dinnertime on a school night, so friend time was officially over. I said no.
He freaked out. He cried. He threw himself on the floor.

After a few minutes of that, I said, "Okay, it's time to stop."

"I can't stop!" he wailed.

I knelt down, looked him in the eye, and cupped my fingers around his arms. "Coleman, your mom cares that you know how to cope. Now let's practice."

Even at seven years old, Coleman had been learning in school about mindfulness and having an anchor spot for calm breathing. We breathed. We talked about focusing his breath on his anchor spot. "I can't do it," he said. We breathed some more. "You can get control," I said. Then after a few more ragged breaths, he did.

Jason and I knew that hard things will happen to Coleman. That's life. As much as we wanted to protect him, we knew we couldn't.

Coleman's best line of defense against unforeseeable difficulties and adversity will be his ability to cope.

His ability to solve a problem.

His ability to adjust when things don't go his way.

His ability to feel his emotions without judgment – even the negative ones.

His ability to let old thoughts go and bring in ones that will help him move forward.

His ability to figure it out.

Because those things will happen.

He'll face problems. He'll experience failures. Friends will abandon him. Some things won't come easily for him. He'll go through pain. He will lose. His heart will break.

His dad will die.

And that's plenty of heartbreak for a ten-year-old, but it probably won't be the last he experiences.

But he will cope. He will be resilient. He will move forward even though it's really hard.

We have a saying in our house. "We're going to roll with it." Ironically appropriate when you live with someone in a wheelchair. For us, that is what resiliency looks like. It's what we say when things don't go our way.

Rolling with it is certainly not our favorite thing to do. How could it be? It's uncomfortable and irritating. We often feel resentful or angry or annoyed that we have to adjust our thinking and actions. But rolling with it is still a path to feeling the positive emotions we're wanting.

I don't mind that Coleman has hard things.
I don't really like that it is *this* particular hard thing, but I don't mind that he has hard things.
I would rather have him go through something difficult now.
With his mom by his side, showing him the way.
So that he can learn how to do it himself.
Because hard things happen. And maybe he'll know how to navigate the next hard thing a little easier because his mom taught him how to roll with this one.

JASON

When life gives you lemons, you're supposed to make lemonade. When life gives you a power wheelchair, you're supposed to give your friends rides and pop wheelies. I didn't want to be known as the guy in a wheelchair. I wanted to be the fun guy who happened to be in a wheelchair. I learned that when it came to my wheelchair, I was happier if I just rolled with it. My mom, on the other hand, probably wanted to strangle me on more than one occasion.

Being a sixteen-year-old with a power wheelchair opened up all sorts of interesting possibilities. There was the morning my brothers and I found an old water ski rope in the garage. We immediately thought of something fun and dangerous to do with it. My brother tied one end of the rope to the back of my chair, and I drove my chair to the middle of the street. Brandon held the rope in his fist and sat in my old manual chair about ten yards behind me.

"Hit it!" he said, and I floored my power chair. I felt a slight tug as the rope tightened, and my chair started pulling Brandon and my old chair behind me. You can imagine the look on my mother's face as she drove into our subdivision and saw me motoring down the street pulling my brother, who was wildly weaving back and forth from sidewalk to sidewalk.

I definitely got a talking to. My mother wasted no time reminding me that my $15,000 power wheelchair was not a toy and should not be treated as such. She warned me of the dangers that could come from messing around with such an expensive piece of equipment. The chair was my responsibility. I promised to be more careful in the future.

In high school, I was very involved in student government. The student officers spent fourth period in leadership class. Leadership class was a time for us to work on our respective student council responsibilities. If we got all our assignments finished, we could fill the time in class any way we wanted. On one of these days when we had too much time on our hands, some of the other officers and I decided to turn my 300-pound motorized wheelchair into a "funny car."

A funny car is a racecar with big wheels in the back and small wheels in the front. When it takes off from the starting line, it has so much horsepower, the front wheels fly off the asphalt. The wheels stay airborne for a few seconds as the car races down the track.

We began to wonder. What would happen if we lined up in the hallway and used every bit of horsepower in my chair while someone simultaneously pulled back as hard as he could on the back of the chair? Would my front wheels lift off the floor? Would I be able to ride all the way down the hall on two wheels?

On the first try, I threw the joystick forward while my friend pulled back on my chair as hard as he could, and for a few feet I rode a "wheelie" down the hall. It was beautiful. We knew if we could go a few feet on our first try, a little more power and a little more pull could take us farther. Again and again we tried, each time going a little farther on just two wheels. The class period was almost over, and we wanted to go out with a bang. We went all the way to the end of the hall to see if I could ride the back wheels the entire length of the hallway. We decided the only way to keep the front wheels up long enough to make it to the end of the hall was to double the weight on the back of my chair.

Two of my friends stood on the back of the chair, hanging onto the handles of my seatback. I gave the joystick all she had. The chair flew forward, and my friends pulled as hard as they could on my seat. Just as the front wheels began to leave the ground, there was a deafening crack.

All that force going opposite directions caused the back of my wheelchair to break off completely. The chair continued to move forward as I fell backwards, my back hitting the ground as I slid completely out of the chair headfirst. My backpack split open, and my books, notepads, and papers scattered across the floor.

The bell rang, and hundreds of kids stepped on, over, and around me to get to lunch. When the hall cleared, my friends helped me get in my backless wheelchair. One of us had the excellent idea to go see the welding teacher. We made our way to the workshop, and he welded my wheelchair back together. The job was good enough to get me home, but not good enough to fool my mother or be a permanent solution.

But I sure had fun rolling with it.

KOLETTE

I design artwork for a company called Silhouette. I create digital files that can be cut out of paper and vinyl and other material using a personal home die-cutting machine. Being one of Silhouette's top designers for years has given me some freedom. I have a healthy portfolio of designs in their online shop. For each design purchased, I get a small royalty.

I like my job. I'm lucky that I work from home, with flexible part-time hours.
People love to craft during the holidays and so October through December is my most profitable time of year.
For seven years, I maximized the opportunity to design for the holiday season.
I cranked out those Halloween and Christmas designs week after week for months.
Make the most of my most lucrative time of year. That was the responsible thing to do.

Then Jason died, and I had a difficult time facing my computer. In the midst of grieving, it was tough to be creative.

Because I was still accruing royalties from past designs, I decided to give myself some time off. Jason died at the end of May. Since the holiday season is the most important time of the year for my business, I made a goal. When school started in

September, I would start designing again.

I didn't design all summer. But it was okay. I'd given myself permission to have a big fat zero in my design submission file.
My goal in September was to do five designs per week.
Five. That's it. I was being realistic, easing into it.
Once October hit, I planned to make the most of the Halloween and Christmas crafting seasons and tackle my maximum of over thirty designs each week.
School started. September pounced on me.
But I still couldn't face the computer.
Adobe Illustrator called to me. Glared at me. Probably said all sorts of mean things behind my back. Unfriended me on Facebook.
I couldn't do it.
I was used to having Jason at home during the day. The house was too quiet. I wandered around, got a snack, watched part of a Hallmark movie, read my book.
My meager goal of creating five designs that week seemed completely out of reach.
I was stuck.
I couldn't sit down at that computer and design anything.

Jason's mom had knee surgery during that time, and one day in the first week of September, I drove her to physical therapy. And took my computer.

I had a theory.

If I put myself in a different environment, maybe I could get unstuck. Maybe I could break through the barrier of inaction I felt at home. Maybe if I put myself in a situation where I could simply *get started*, then I could keep going.

Thursday, September 5.
We got to the physical therapist.
I pulled out my computer.
Forty-five minutes later, I had a design plan.
And one image done.

That night, I finished five more.
Six designs submitted that first week.
Five is awesome.
Six makes me a rock star.

But grieving is harder than I thought it would be.
My newfound enthusiasm didn't last long.
I didn't create another design the rest of the month.

October rolled around, and I was still struggling.
I did those six designs the first week of September, preparing to ramp up for full production in October.
But my problem was still there. The barrier. The struggle to sit at the computer.

"I should work," I thought.
"It's the holidays.
The Black Friday sale is coming.
I have to maximize this time of year.
I should work."

Then, this next question floated into my mind.

"But should I work? Really?
Just because it's what I've always done, do I have to do it this year?
Is it okay to choose differently than what I'm used to choosing?"

I wasn't sure.

Wasn't making the most of my holiday work the responsible thing to do?
It became an inner battle as my sense of responsibility tangled with our current needs.
I prayed about it. Often.
I thought about it. Always.
Then I got an idea. An impression.
It was clear.
It was personal.
It was full of peace.
"It's okay to not work right now," the thought said.

I began to test this idea for its truthfulness as more thoughts floated through my head.
The worst possible event has actually happened.
Just because I have always worked, doesn't necessarily mean I have to now.
We have what we need.
I can choose something different than what I have always done.

"It's ok to not work right now," had been my thought.
And that thought was telling the truth.

Peace.
That's what I began to feel.
Peace that Coleman and I were cared for.
Peace that I had choices.
Peace that I could navigate my new normal differently.
Peace that Coleman wouldn't have his mom stuck behind a computer for three months during the holidays.
Peace so I could grieve and feel and heal.
And when the time is right, I'll decide what work will look like for me.

Sometimes rolling with it means changing our pattern so that we can get started.

Sometimes rolling with it means being brave enough to completely change what we have always done. New circumstances might require a new solution.

And we're just going to roll with it.

JASON

Before I broke my neck, I loved to dance. In Boise, there was a church youth group dance every Saturday night for all the fourteen-, fifteen-, and sixteen-year-olds. We called it the SND—Saturday Night Dance. During those years, the worst threat my parents could make was to warn me that if I didn't do my chores, I couldn't go to the SND. I would do nearly anything to attend the Saturday Night Dance.

After I broke my neck, I stayed away from formal dating and dancing. I'd never seen anybody go on a formal date in a wheelchair, and I'd never seen anybody dance in a wheelchair. I didn't know if it could be done, so I simply stayed away. By my junior year, I was going to high school full time again and had been elected junior class president. Part of my responsibilities was to go to school activities. One of the first big activities was the Homecoming dance.

Weeks before the dance, my friends started asking me who I was going take to Homecoming. I came up with a dozen excuses. My friends refused to let me live my life any differently in a wheelchair, and I knew if I told them I was too scared to go, they would show up at my house on the night of the dance, lift me out of bed, throw me into the car in my pajamas, and ask a stranger off the street to be my date.

As scared as I was to go to the dance, I was more scared of my friends. Finally I told them I was going to be out of town the night of the dance. On the night of the dance, I drove to Meridian, which from where I lived in Boise was about two-and-a-half minutes roundtrip on your elbows. You could spit to Meridian from my house. But I was still technically "out of town" and had pretty much told my friends the truth. The next week at school, everybody had pictures from the dance. I wanted a picture so bad. I didn't even care if I was in the picture, I just wanted to be part of the group.

The next dance at my school was the Harvest Hop. It's a girl-ask-guy dance where the couple wears matching shirts so they can be "twinners." I was sure I was safe. What girl was going to ask a guy in a wheelchair? But one day I came home to find a basket on my doorstep. The basket was full of clues for me to follow and puzzles to put together. At the end of it all, I discovered that my friend Karen wanted to go to the dance with me. I was excited and answered her with a resounding, "Yes!"

It wasn't long before I began to have second thoughts. "You don't know how to dance." Instant fear! "What have I done?" I panicked. The next day I found out Karen had bought short-sleeved shirts for us to wear to the dance. I sighed in relief. I had a perfect excuse not to go to the dance with her. "Karen," I said, "November is too cold for short-sleeved shirts. Let's just skip it." Karen listened to my concerns, but by the end of the conversation, we were still going to the dance.

Every week, I came up with a new and imaginative reason we shouldn't go, but Karen wasn't having any of it. She refused to let me wheedle my way out of going to the dance. The day before the dance, I took drastic measures. "Karen, let's just not go!" I said. She looked at me and said, "Shut up and go." To which I replied, "Yes, ma'am."

That was before I had my handicap-accessible van, so when the night of the dance came around, I couldn't drive myself. Karen came to pick me up in her cute little Toyota Tercel. My wheelchair wouldn't fit in the back, so she had to return home and get her mom's Country Squire station wagon. It was an enormous car. It took four blocks just to parallel park that bad boy.

At the dance, the line for pictures seemed a mile long. Karen suggested we go in and dance and maybe the line for pictures would get shorter. I said, "No. Let's get pictures now," hoping that by the time we got through the picture line, the dance would be over. Unfortunately, we got pictures taken, and there was plenty of dance left. I was forced to make some attempt to dance in my wheelchair. The first song was a fast one and not knowing what else to do, I clapped my hands to the rhythm. By the second song, I felt a little bit better and moved my arms a little more to the beat. The third song got better still, and by the fourth song, there was a group of people around me, calling out my name, cheering me on to dance. I was getting into it.

But then it happened. A slow song. "Punch bowl. Get to the punch bowl!" I thought. I turned that wheelchair of mine around and headed to the refreshment table as fast as I could. Karen grabbed the back of my wheelchair, spun me around, jumped on my lap, and put her arm around me. "Let's dance," she said. I thought that was a great idea. In fact, when the slow song ended, I was thinking we should dance all of the dances like that.

When I think about that night, I often ask, "Why was Karen willing to go through all of that just to take me to the dance?" She didn't get to drive the coolest car to the dance. It was so huge that they could have fit the refreshment table in that thing. She had to lift me in and out of the car all night—into the car at my house, out of the car at the restaurant, in at the restaurant, out at the dance, in at the dance, out at my house. She had long pretty hair that was curled and nice for the dance, but after all that lifting, it got sweaty and straight, not the way she wanted to show up to the dance. I wasn't the most popular kid in my school. No one was asking, "Hey, I wonder who gets to take Jason Hall to the dance."

But Karen cared. She was willing to cut through all of my excuses. I'd never gone to a dance with a date, but she'd never taken a guy in a wheelchair to a dance. She'd certainly never had to lift her date in and out of the car before or sit in order to dance. Karen never gave up. She was willing to roll with it that night, and I learned that I could too.

KOLETTE

I take Coleman and his cousins to ski at our local resort almost every weekend during the winter. My sister-in-law and I share carpool duties and each take one way.

As we got in the car one Saturday morning during spring skiing, I gave Coleman the weather report. "So, it's been kind of rainy. It might be a little slushy today."

With unbounded enthusiasm, Coleman replied, "Mom, I do not care about the conditions! I just want to go skiing."

Karen didn't seem to care about the conditions either when she decided to take Jason to a dance. She faced barriers and obstacles at every turn. Who wants to hang in there when your date keeps saying, "Let's just not go?"

But she did hang in there. She did keep going.
And because she did, Jason never missed another school dance.

JASON

At one time, I was in the hospital for a three-month stay. Every day the therapists put me in my chair, and I had two hours to go anywhere I wanted inside the hospital. For liability reasons, I wasn't allowed to leave the hospital, so my therapists never took the time to get me fully dressed for my two-hour excursions. I wore a hospital gown that went to my knees...barely. They wrapped one giant towel around my top half and another around my bottom half. Not stylish, but it covered me up.

I went everywhere in the hospital. I'd go down to X-ray, over to the helipad, get some grilled cheese in the cafeteria, and check out the Hummel figurines in the gift shop. After three weeks, I'd pretty much seen everything twice. I got bored. I decided that the next time they got me in my chair, I was going to defy protocol and bust out of the hospital for an afternoon.

I was really into comic books, and Wednesday was the day the new comic books were available at the comic book store. Usually my mom or Kolette picked up my standing comic book order and brought it to me in the hospital. That Wednesday, I decided I was going to go to the store myself and get my own comic books.

The therapists and nurses put me in my chair, wrapped me up, and let me go, not suspecting my cunning but brilliant plan. I went to the lobby and waited for my chance. The hospital security guard at the front door had two jobs—keep the crazies out and keep the crazies in—and this guard was incredibly vigilant. I waited for him to get distracted or look away, but he never wavered in his duty.

The comic store was two miles away from the hospital, and I was on the clock. I was coming to a Go—No-Go decision. Either I made a break for it or slouched back to my room in defeat.

I happened to be listening to the song "Falls Apart" in my headphones. "Run away, run away," Sugar Ray coaxed. That was all the inspiration I needed. I drove my wheelchair to the door and tried to look like I was on my way to a business appointment—wrapped in two giant towels. I don't know if the security guard didn't see me or just had pity on me, but I made it out the door without being stopped.

There aren't a lot of sidewalks in Connecticut, so I cruised down the street as close to the side as I could. Near misses from cars whizzing by only added to the adventure.

About halfway to the comic book store, I hit a bump in the road, jostling my chair and shaking the bottom towel loose. A corner of the towel got caught in the wheel, and suddenly, the towel was gone. I don't know how much of me was showing, but I do know breezes were blowing on parts of my body where they hadn't blown before.

At that point, I was faced with a choice. Did I keep going to the comic book store or did I head back to the hospital? Man, I wanted those comic books, and I wanted to get them myself, half-dressed or not.

I kept going. When I got to the store, I checked myself in the window to make sure I wasn't going to get arrested for exposure. The guy at the register gave me my comics and a funny look, and I headed back to the hospital.

I don't know that I have ever enjoyed reading my comics as much as I did that evening. Each page had joy emanating from it. There's something special about really having to work hard to earn something, about being so determined, so "Comic Book Committed" that you cannot be deterred from the finish line. Your wheels cannot be stopped. You just have to keep going. The reward for being Comic Book Committed is far sweeter than the price printed on the cover.

KOLETTE

Jason and I got married knowing we would probably need help to have a baby. We first tried artificial insemination.

For two years, I took medication for ovulation.
We calculated days on the calendar.
We tested the timing.
We traveled long distances for procedures.
We gathered Jason's contribution in a sterile hospital room.
We spent money that stretched our newly-married budget.

It didn't work.

In the fall of 1997, we met with a new fertility specialist and made plans to start IVF (in vitro fertilization) the following January—as soon as we had the funds to make it happen.

On November 27, Jason's front tire blew, and his thirteen-month stay in the hospital began. Along with Jason's van, our baby plans came to a screeching halt. Over the next ten years, Jason had approximately thirty surgeries. He was in and out of the hospital constantly.

Fifteen years after we were married, with over a decade of rehabilitation and recovery behind us, Jason was healthy enough to try again.

We weren't sure it would work.
I was thirty-six years old, now considered "high risk" because of my age. The doctor said my eggs were old and depleting.
Jason's sperm had even lower motility than it had eleven years earlier.
Our chances weren't good.

Because Jason couldn't use his hands, I gave myself the required daily injections of fertility medications.

My body changed. It adjusted to the prescriptions I pumped into it to release as many eggs as possible on the day of retrieval.

The hope and fear, longing and uncertainty, were overwhelming.

"Keep your stress to a minimum," the doctor said.

How is that even possible when your dreams are riding on procedures that cost thousands of dollars and the unpredictable response of your body?

We did our best to stay calm.

To laugh together.

To not put pressure on ourselves.

To be positive.

To remind ourselves that whatever happened, it would be ok.

To remember that God has his hand in all things.

But it was still stressful. Still really hard.

On the day of retrieval I had produced nine eggs.

The fertilization specialists planned to fertilize each egg individually and let them grow into, hopefully, eight-celled embryos. They would freeze some and place some in my womb to see if they would create a viable pregnancy.

There was one problem.

When the doctor tried to gather Jason's sperm, because of his years of paralysis, there wasn't any to gather.

My doctor didn't give up. "There's something we can try," he said. "It requires us to take a biopsy to see if we can find any sperm in Jason's tissue."

The biopsy was Jason's decision, but I knew what he'd tell the doctor. "Whatever it takes. Do the biopsy." Keep rolling forward.

That evening we got a call from the clinic.

"We found eleven sperm. But they're not moving. We're going to try to wake them up."

Wake them up? We were dismayed that they had to do this but amazed that it was actually possible.

After a sleepless night, wondering, hoping, praying for a miracle, we received another call.

"It worked. We've fertilized nine eggs." With eleven sperm.

Inexpressible joy washed over us. The doctors hadn't tried to implant an embryo yet, but we already recognized the miracles in this journey.

To have the best chance for survival, each embryo needed to develop to the eight-cell stage.

Six out of nine embryos made it through the fertilization process.

A few days later, our doctor implanted the three best embryos in my uterus.

We waited two weeks then took the blood test to determine if I was pregnant.

I wasn't.

After all of the miracles, it hadn't worked.

Our disappointment was bitter, as anyone knows who has gone through it.

A lost chance.

Grief hung over us.

We had to wait three months to try again.

Three last embryos taken from the freezer.

Our last chance before we would have to start the process all over again, not knowing if we could even get more sperm from Jason.

Two weeks and another blood test later, the phone call came.

"You're pregnant!" Those are the two happiest words we have ever heard.

Coleman Jason Hall was born on January 27, 2009, eleven years after we had originally planned to start IVF and sixteen years into our marriage.

Coleman was a miracle, but it never would have happened without the grit and determination of each person involved. No one gave up. Jason was committed to do whatever it took to be a father. The doctor was willing to try a different procedure. The staff adapted when faced with something new. The fertilization specialist persevered even when reaching our goal felt impossible.

I know what it's like to long for a child.
I know the ache of Mother's Day.
I know how it feels when your best friend or your neighbor or your sister-in-law announces she's pregnant, again.
I know how to take a deep breath and feel genuine joy for her when I really want to cry for myself.
I know that the gift of a healthy, full-term pregnancy doesn't happen for everyone. We recognize the miracle.

I was diagnosed with gallstone pancreatitis fifteen months after Coleman was born.
The surgeon had to rebuild my abdomen.
I would never be able to sustain a pregnancy again.
For months I was too sick to care for my one child, let alone have another one.
Trying to adopt wasn't in the cards with my weakened physical health.

Infertility is a heartbreak all its own. It's grieving the loss of what is possible.
Our story very easily could have gone another way.

We are grateful that we stuck it out years after we made our plan to pursue IVF.
We are grateful that we had people around us who were willing to keep rolling forward with us.
But what if it hadn't worked? After all of that time and all of that money, what if it hadn't worked?

Being resilient requires something of us.

Life is packed with opportunities to practice coping, to practice adjusting, to practice resilience.

Tough stuff is going to happen, and unexpected challenges will arise. Plans will be made that won't work like we think they should. Bumps in the road that jostle our lives are a sure thing. Boulders in our path will seem insurmountable.

But we are the Halls.

We choose to be Comic Book Committed.

We figure out a solution.

We find a new way.

We keep moving forward.

In spite of the hard things, we're just going to keep rolling with it.

FACEBOOK POST – JANUARY 24, 2020 (DAY 245)

Since Jason died, cooking has been beyond my capability level and so I tend to do what is easiest.
Mindless grab-and-go food.

But that had to change.
In October I started on an ultra-simple plan to adjust my food intake.
And I walked.
Every day but Sunday.
I walked at least 15,000 steps.

I've always tried to exercise but this was new to me.
I bought an Apple Watch to track my progress.
I walked around the neighborhood.
I walked around the field during Coleman's lacrosse practice.
I braved the busy, no-sidewalk stretch of road and walked to Walmart.

Winter came.
I almost fell on the ice. Twice.
I bought a treadmill and put it in my room.
Because that's where I'd use it most.

I've become the weird walking lady.
Walking everywhere.
Heidi drove by. "I've seen you walking the neighborhood three times today!"
Every year I choose a word.
I'm not a resolution maker, although I do set goals.
I just don't set them in the pressure-filled days of January. They happen when I choose.
Instead, at the beginning of each of the last twelve years, I pick a word.
Each time a different word bubbles to the surface and calls out to me.
Then it just lingers on the edges of my choices throughout the year, quietly encouraging me to allow it space to teach me.

This year I struggled to find the right word.
A word holding little expectation for this tender, grieving widow.
Then I realized that I say my word at least a dozen times a day.

Step.
That's my word.
And yes, I mean my 15,000 walking steps.
The chance to move and be outside, think my thoughts and feel peace.
But what else is it?

I don't have grand plans or big dreams to accomplish this year.
No. I'm thinking much smaller.
I simply want to listen to personal revelation, recognize it for what it is, and take the step needed to act on it.
Maybe it'll be some big steps.
Most likely it will be tiny ones.

But when I feel like something is right, I just want to have the faith and courage to take a little action.
To take a little step.

I walk to the cemetery.
I walk to the hardware store.
I walk everywhere these days.
Pam went to Disneyland and looked at her steps. "Kolette does this every day!"
Looks like every day is a Disneyland day around here.
Step.

Come walk with me?

CHAPTER 6
JASON WILL DO ANYTHING
FOR A SLURPEE

I came home last night to fresh cucumbers and tomatoes on my porch.

The afternoon before Jason died, he and his aide planted the garden.
I'm not a gardener.
That was Jason's thing.
I'm the eater of the fresh garden tomatoes.

Over the years, Jason tried a few plants, learned some things, tried new stuff.
Each year he had a plan of how that year was going to be even better than last.

And he was usually right (except for the pesky red peppers that eluded him).

We had garden boxes built along the south side of the house for easy wheelchair access along his cobblestone path.

Coleman and the aide became his partners as they watered daily, tied vines to cages, nurtured, and coaxed each little plant.

He tried sweet peas and cantaloupe,
Cucumbers and jalapeños and red peppers,

His babies, though, were always his beloved tomatoes.

*He figured out that a plant combo of Early Girls and Best Boys gave
us the flavor we wanted over the longest harvest time.*

*Sunsweets were our favorite cherry tomato. We ate them sprinkled
liberally with salt by the bowlful.*

Bacon and tomato sandwiches four times a week? Yes, please!

We had plenty of tomatoes to share with neighbors too.

*Jason always connected with the workers at the garden shops,
Asked for advice,
Got good tips on what bug was causing a certain black blotch or
what to do for the tomatoes that had dry, brown spots on them.*

*Jason couldn't find the Sunsweets this year.
Two weeks after he died, a dear lady left a message on his phone:
"Jason, it's Patti from J&J. I was just at the Cal-Ranch, and they had
six Sunsweets in. I thought you would want to know."*

*I called Patti back, told her the news,
Thanked her for caring for Jason.
She cried with me because Jason was her friend,
The guy in the wheelchair who loved his garden.*

*I had my first bacon and tomato sandwich of the summer last night.
With Jason's tomato.
Deep red.
That flavor!
Juicy.*

Seriously. You just can't find that at the store.

Thanks, Amber, for your tireless service in tending to Jason's garden this year.
I just couldn't do it.
Couldn't even walk out to his garden, really.
You're my neighbor, but you have gone beyond being "neighborly" this summer.

Thanks for the gorgeous gift on my doorstep.
I hope you took some home for yourself!

JASON

From the day I received my power wheelchair, it has been my responsibility to ensure that my chair is plugged in at night. Although someone else has to actually plug the chair in, it is my job to make sure it gets done so the batteries are recharged by morning.

Every once in a while, I forget to ask someone to plug in my chair. The first time I forgot was during my junior year of high school. Forgetting my chair hadn't been plugged in the night before, I went to school as usual, but during second period, I noticed the reading on the power meter—half full. Usually at that time of day my chair was still showing full charge. I was a little concerned but hoped half a "tank" would be enough to get me home.

Unfortunately, the meter continued to fall as the day went on. By lunchtime I barely had an eighth of a charge left. I started to conserve every bit of energy I still had in my chair. I didn't go outside to hang out with my friends during lunch. I didn't go to my locker. I took the most direct routes to my classes.

By the end of the final period, I was running on empty. I could barely manage a crawl with the power I had left. I thought maybe I had conserved enough energy that, with a little luck, I could make it to my van outside. Knowing how long it would take me to get to my van, I left class fifteen minutes early. I exited the school and rolled slowly down the sidewalk. My chair was hungry for power, and the motor sounded like the moan of a sick animal. I reached the road and saw my van just across the street. I was almost home free.

I inched across the road, but at least I was moving. Unfortunately, road engineering proved my downfall. When they pave roads, they often grade them with a slight decline on each side so rain will run off the road and into the gutters on either side.

The grade on the road wasn't steep, but it was too steep for a wheelchair low on power. Getting up the scant incline used the rest of the battery. When I got to the middle of the road, my chair was completely out of juice. The lights on my hand control shut off. I sat in the middle of the road with no way to get to my van. Even though I'd left class early, it had taken me so long to get to the road that school was out, and all those distracted high school drivers were getting into their cars.

As I sat in the middle of the road, I heard a roar that made the ground rumble. I turned to see what was coming my way. One of my classmates barreled down the road in his 1975 muscle car made of one hundred percent Detroit steel. He'd blown past the school-zone sign at well over the prescribed 20 mph. His radio was turned up beyond any legal decibel level while his arm and his attention were wrapped around his girlfriend instead of the road. That was when I really started to panic.

The Jason Hall Story flashed before my eyes.

The final chapter of my life played across my mind, ending with a scene in which my chair and body flew through the air in opposite directions.

In an instant, someone came up behind me, shoved my chair into neutral, and pushed me out of the way. My friend James pushed me off the road in the nick of time. The car missed us by the smallest of margins. We could feel the rush of air as the driver passed, never realizing how close he'd come to putting a very large dent in his beloved car.

We stopped to catch our breath, then James and another friend pushed my chair into my van so I could drive home.

James knew I was stuck. He knew how to put my chair in neutral so he could move me out of the way. That's what happens when someone serves us. Service sees a need, knows how to help, and gets us unstuck.

Sometimes we're stuck in a thought or attitude that isn't working. Sometimes we're stuck in a place we can't escape, a hard thing, a challenge, a tough spot. Other times, we're the ones who know how to solve a problem for someone else.

And maybe the one who knows how to push us across the road is just waiting for us to be willing to take the help.

KOLETTE

Before Jason's car accident that landed him in the hospital for thirteen months, we were strong and independent.
We had been married for five years.
We had a medical aide who came in every morning and night to perform Jason's personal care, getting him dressed and lifting him in and out of his chair.

I was in charge of everything else.
I kept the house clean and organized so Jason's chair didn't run over shoes or jackets or my purse.

I cooked all the meals, did all the dishes.
Scrubbed the toilets and sinks.
Vacuumed and did the laundry.
Jason did the shopping because it was something he could help with.

He worked hard as a financial planner and earned a spot in the Million Dollar Round Table, among the top six percent in his industry, every year.
He got up at 6:00 a.m. His personal care took two hours.
After his aide left, he had breakfast appointments, lunch appointments, dinner appointments, and called referrals to set more appointments in between.
He got home late and was in bed by 11:00 p.m.
He gave motivational speeches to corporations and youth groups about overcoming and positivity and perseverance.
Jason was a hard worker.

Even with all he'd been through, he had never experienced depression.

Then things changed.
He started feeling a pain in his abdomen. They called it neuro-logical pain and couldn't find the source. He didn't have feeling in his abdomen, but he was suddenly experiencing pain.

Pain is a ruthless thing.
It can start to take over your entire thought process.
Rob you of the ability to feel joy, move forward, and see the good.
That's what happened to Jason.

The pain led to discouragement, which led to depression.
Jason, who got going early—making the sale and working harder than anyone—couldn't do it anymore.

I left to teach school every morning.
He figured out how to shift himself out of his chair and onto the

sofa. He couldn't get back into his chair so he stayed on the sofa. All day.

He would call me every day at 3:30 p.m. sharp. "Where are you?"
"I'm on my way home. Just like always."
This was a Jason I never knew.
He was the positive guy. The one who kept going even when it was hard.
The guy who worked his guts out to achieve a goal.
The guy who never quit.
Pain had hijacked his life.

JASON

I was admitted into the hospital so the doctors could do a series of tests to try and discover the cause of my pain. Later as I lay in my hospital bed, a stranger came into my room. He asked me about my disability and what strategies I used to stay positive.

I had talked about these principles in speeches so often I rattled them off without thinking:

Face adversity with a happy heart!
Keep going even when life is hard!
Have faith!
Believe that it's possible!
See the good!
Be grateful!
Find humor in everything!
Surround yourself with positives!
Work hard!
Persevere!
Never give up!

"Are you doing those things now?" he asked. I was offended and a little annoyed. Who was he to ask me that question? He showed me his nametag and introduced himself as a member of the hospital psychology team. Kolette and my doctor had asked him to assess my mental health. I was irritated that anyone thought I needed this kind of help and fumed that they had gone behind my back. When I was alone again, I considered his question. Had I slipped? Was I doing as well as I thought I was?

Later, I went to see that psychiatrist. He reminded me that I needed to take those strategies I preached about and use them to help me with this new challenge called pain. Life is like that. Just when we figure out how to overcome a hard thing, something else happens, a different hard, and we have to figure it out all over again.

Remembering and reapplying time-tested strategies was what I needed to get back on track. I stopped sitting on the sofa all day. I got back to work. I was on the upswing with my life. We hadn't told anyone except my doctor about those dark days. We just worked through it and kept going because we thought we could totally do this ourselves.

I didn't want to let anyone help me more than they were already helping. I didn't want to burden anyone. My medical aide assisted me in the mornings and evenings, but I was relatively independent. At family events, I didn't want others to fill my plate or get me a drink or help me find a place to eat because I wanted to do things myself. Which really meant Kolette would be the one to do it.

So she did. Kolette did it all. She sincerely believed that if she truly loved me, she should be able to do everything for me. She thought that was what good caregivers did. Then my front tire blew, and I started a thirteen-month stay in the hospital. By that time, she was exhausted. Kolette was feeling the burden of my "independence."

KOLETTE

When Jason had his car accident in 1992, we thought he was going to die. Our church leader came to the house. "It's time you let people help."
The day of Jason's accident, I came home to a home-cooked meal from a dear neighbor. I was in shock, and the thought of all that food overwhelmed me.

I would be spending many days at the hospital, days where we were just trying to survive. My neighbors wanted to help.
A plan was made.
A neighborhood sign-up sheet was organized.
Whatever they had for dinner that night, they made a plate for me.
They put it in my Winder Dairy box on the porch each night by 6:00 p.m.

Most of the time I wasn't home by 6:00, so I rarely knew who had left the meal that day. When I said my prayers, I asked God to bless the family who had brought me dinner, whoever it was.

I never saw the sign-up sheet.
No one ever claimed responsibility for that night's meal.
I never had a person inform me they had brought dinner over the night before.
For almost six months, I went to my porch, opened my dairy box, and found a full plate. Almost 200 dinners.

My neighbors were the stick-it-out kind of givers.

About two months into Jason's hospital stay, I told Jason's mom, "Maybe I should tell them to stop bringing meals. I feel like I should be able to do it."

"It's the only meal you are eating each day," she said. "You're losing weight. Let them bring the food." So I let them.

And that wasn't all they did.

At the beginning of December, someone strung Christmas lights on our house. I pulled up to the house, sat in the driveway, and wept.

A friend purchased all the supplies for a Mother's Day project for my fourth grade class and brought them to me with assembly instructions. I wouldn't have been able to do that myself. I just didn't have the emotional energy.

There were countless visits to the hospital.
Lawns mowed.
Sprinklers fixed.
Broken doors, latches, drawers, and dishwashers repaired.
Walks in the park.
Chats on the front porch.
Letters and pictures for Jason's room.
Invitations to activities so I wouldn't be alone.
Bench partners at church.

A couple of weeks into Jason's ICU stay, I was coming down off the initial stress and feeling the weight of what we were facing. He had broken almost every bone in his body. His head had thirty-five stitches. His mouth was battered and swollen. And he was a quadriplegic. Healing from his injuries was going to be slow.
I was twenty-six years old and completely overwhelmed.
Exhaustion from caregiving had chipped away at me.
I felt completely defeated.
My shoulders slumped as I sat at our little kitchen table. The one we bought at a discount in the furniture store basement when we first got married.
"Maybe I should just leave," I thought.
"This wasn't the plan.
I'm so tired. I don't think I can do this."

The feeling settled into my bones as I seriously considered walking away.

Walking away from the hospital.

Walking away from being a caregiver.

Walking away from Jason's injuries.

Walking away from the burden. The weight. The heaviness of it all.

I called Jason's dad, Stephen. We are close, and at that moment of crisis, I needed to talk to someone who loved Jason as much as I did, someone who understood what it was like to be a caregiver. Someone who might relate to what I was feeling.

"Dad, I'm in trouble."

I told Stephen about Jason's earlier depression. I told him how we had tried to do everything by ourselves. That independence Jason and I so proudly clung to had worn me out.

I was tired, discouraged, ashamed.

The guilt of not being there for Jason, not doing it all, was overwhelming.

I just knew that I was not doing enough. Not being enough. Not good enough.

On the tailcoats of guilt, bitterness seeped in.

Not only did I think that I was not enough, but I didn't even want to be enough.

I didn't want to do it.

The hospital.

The watching my husband cling to every breath.

The surgeries.

The waiting.

The wondering if he would be alive tomorrow.

Resentment and Anger had partnered with their friend Guilt, and they took turns pushing at me in their game of "You are Not Enough."

I didn't want to do any of it, but at the same time, I felt terrible about feeling that way.

"You have to let go of the guilt," Stephen told me.

Tears fell as I admitted, "I don't know how."

That began my tutorial from Stephen.
My lesson came in the form of my own set of chore cards.
Things I had to do each day.
But the chore cards Stephen gave to me that day looked different than the ones he had brought to a fifteen-year-old boy eleven years earlier.

They were custom. Meant for a twenty-six-year-old girl who loved his son but wasn't sure if she could do it anymore.
By this time, I was teaching half days. The school had hired another teacher to be with my class so that I could go to the hospital in the afternoons.

Here's what my chores looked like:
1. I could visit Jason in the hospital but I had to leave by 3:30 p.m., just like I would have if it had been a normal school day.
2. I could only stay at the hospital for one hour.
3. At the hospital, I wasn't allowed to help Jason. No handing him a drink of water or adjusting his bed. I could hit the call button, talk with him, and sit by his side.

That's it. Stephen purposefully removed caregiving responsibilities from my shoulders.
Sounds pretty harsh, right? Looking back, it probably was harsh.
I never would have chosen those rules on my own.
Guilt would have reigned supreme.

I was seriously looking at the option of walking away.
I was being sucked into the mire of guilt and resentment that comes from fear of failing.
Failing at caring for my husband enough.
Failing at loving him enough.
Failing at being enough.
As Jason fought for his life on a breathing machine in the ICU, I believed that I was a caregiving failure.

Those chore cards helped me take a second chance on my marriage.

Jason's parents arranged for others to be at the hospital with Jason. I worked to let go of the guilt for not being there all the time. Family members took shifts doing things to help Jason. Jason had plenty of care. Just not from me.

Did I feel guilty? You bet.
Stephen talked with Jason to fill him in on my chores.
He knew we were doing the best we could. But he also knew that we had to learn a new way of handling our challenges or our marriage might not survive.

"You can't do this anymore," Stephen said.
"You have to let other people besides Kolette help you.
It's not her job.
Independence might cost you your wife.
You can do this. We'll help you."

I went to the hospital every day, but not stepping in to help Jason was hard. Feeling guilty for just sitting there and letting others do everything was hard.
But I also knew that I was teetering on the edge of completely giving up.

The weeks moved on. I got stronger.
I could help arrange his blanket without anger flaring up inside my chest.
I could help him eat his lunch without animosity roaring through my head.
I could help place the straw to his mouth when he asked for a drink and even began offering it to him without being asked.
The anger and bitterness faded.

As months passed, my thoughts began to change. Guilt was slowly replaced by a lesson. A testimony of my own. Starting out as a tiny ember but gaining fuel as I began to open my heart to different feelings. The alternate options of forgiveness, compassion, empathy, peace, and love. For Jason and for myself.

It takes strength to let go of guilt.
It takes courage to say, "Doing everything does not make me a better wife or a better mother or a better person."

I was learning that I am brave when I sift through my responsibilities with a critical eye.
When I choose my expectations based on how they will affect myself, my family, and those I care about.
Guilt is an easy but dangerous companion, as it stands haughtily on a foundation of judgment and criticism.
I heard the comments from others:
"You should be sleeping at the hospital so you're with him all the time."
"Shouldn't you be doing more for him by now?"
"If I were Kolette, I would…"

Well-meaning people are very good at handing guilt to us. Giving us that simmering, toxic gift wrapped up in a suggestion or opinion full of things we should and should not be doing. We are very good at heaping that same criticism on ourselves.
But maybe there is a different story.
Maybe I could let people help.
Maybe it wasn't all up to me.
Maybe my burden of guilt wasn't required after all.
Maybe I could set it down. Let it go.
Maybe I was exactly enough.

There's something powerful about letting someone else set the rules.
Stephen's chore cards gave me permission.

Permission to view my self-expectations differently.
Permission to see that there might be a better way.
Permission to show up just as I was and let others lend a hand.
Permission to decide to stay.

JASON

After the car accident, I lay flat in bed, and I didn't sit in my chair for months. My physical therapist told me I had to learn how to sit up.

"Learn to sit up? I've been sitting up most of my life. I know I've been through a bad stretch here, but this has just been a few months. I think I can sit up."

"Okay, smart guy," the therapist said. The therapists lifted me out of my bed and into my wheelchair. I immediately passed out, and they put me back in bed. I swallowed my pride and admitted that I was going to have to learn to sit up again. The therapist didn't even say, "I told you so."

When you lie in bed long enough, your lungs settle, and they don't know how to work when you're upright. I couldn't sit up.

I started practicing sitting up. They'd put me in the wheelchair for ten seconds then back to my bed. After a few days, I worked up to fifteen seconds then thirty. Thirty seconds turned into a minute, then five, then ten. After a few weeks, I was able to sit in my chair for an hour. It was a great accomplishment, but I didn't—couldn't—stop there. Unfortunately, I couldn't sit up longer than an hour. Every time I got to an hour, I became really short of breath, and they'd have to put me back in bed.

My care center had a walkway running alongside a river. Every day when the weather was a nice, my therapist took me for a walk by the river. One day, I could tell we were reaching my hour limit. "Kelly, I can't make it. I've got to go back."

"Jason, at the end of this path, there's a 7-11. If you can get to the 7-11, I'll buy you a Slurpee."

I don't know how many of you have spent months at a time in the hospital, but when you can get a Slurpee, it's like Ambrosia. It was impossible for me to imagine something I might want more than a Slurpee, and so I agreed to move ahead.

I got my cherry Slurpee—best Slurpee flavor ever—and we headed back to my room. As I finished my Slurpee, I looked up at the clock. It had been an hour and a half! Distracted by the promise of a Slurpee, I had busted through my previous record.

Every day we walked along that path, Kelly would buy me a Slurpee. Every day he'd walk just a little slower. An hour turned into an hour and half, which turned into two, which turned into three.

I don't know the details of your health insurance coverage, but mine didn't pay for a therapist to take three hours to walk me to 7-11 every day. Kelly gave up breaks, lunches, and days off so he could walk me down that path. Other therapists gave up their breaks and their lunches covering for Kelly so he could walk with me down that path. Kelly changed my life with compassion and kindness in the form of a Slurpee.

What Slurpee have you given someone today?

KOLETTE

Jason had to ask for help all day, every day of his life. Maybe that's why we fought so hard to be independent.

But were we really independent?
Sort of.

Independence is definitely good. We needed to be self-reliant and have skills to care for ourselves. But we also had resources we chose not to tap into. We had people we could have talked to about Jason's pain and bout with depression, family members who would have offered support and tools. Friends who would have understood and been there for us.
Not using those resources closed us off.
In an effort to be independent, our focus turned to ourselves.
It was all about our own strength. Our own capability.

Accepting service required us to turn outward.

To open our minds.
To open our hearts.
To open our arms.

It's hard to do. To be a little vulnerable.
Sometimes we think, "It's great if I serve others, but no way should I need anyone to serve me."

I thought that too.
Until I almost walked out on the man I love because we were trying to do it all ourselves.
Being independent sounds like a good idea. And sometimes it is. But sometimes it keeps us from accepting the exact thing that we need most. Like a Slurpee.

JASON

One night, when Coleman was about five years old, Kolette had to be at a meeting.
It was my job to take care of Coleman that night. I went into

Epic Dad Mode and decided to do Boys Night Out. We were going to get hamburgers, go bowling, get ice cream, and play video games. The whole everything!

After that, he'd be nice and tired, and I would have no trouble getting him into bed.

On her way out the door, Kolette said, "Jason, just so you know, Coleman hasn't been feeling very well so you may want to take it easy."

"He looks fine," I thought, in classic dad fashion. "We're going to go out and have a great time."

I proceeded with the plan. It was a great night. We ate hamburgers and ice cream. We both bowled excellent games. When we came home, Coleman took two steps into our house and threw up all over the floor. It was horrible. Hamburger, ice cream, bowling balls. Everything we had done that night pooled on the kitchen floor. He ran into the bathroom, knelt at the toilet, and threw up again, but he had gone into the one bathroom in our home that I can't get into. There I was, stuck outside his bathroom watching him cry. "Coleman, come here. Let me help you. Let me fix this."

He wouldn't come to me. He just sat there and cried into the toilet. It was gut-wrenching and painful. I knew how to help him, but I couldn't get him to come. I never felt more disabled in my life. All my heart wanted was to help this boy that I loved so much, and I couldn't get him to come. Finally, he came to me. I helped him get cleaned up, wrapped him in a blanket, got him some medicine, and put him to bed. Five minutes later, he was asleep.

There are times when hard things happen, and we feel the same way Coleman did, even if we're not keen on crying next to the toilet. Still, all we want to do is cry, complain, be sad, be upset at how rotten life is. We think we should solve everything by ourselves. All the while, I think Jesus Christ, our friend and brother, stands there saying, "Come here. Let me help you. Let me bless you." All we have to do is come.

He knows exactly how to love us, how to succor us, how to bless us. But He can't do it if we don't ask, and He can't help if we don't turn toward Him.

KOLETTE

Jason did the grocery shopping in our house, even after we had Coleman. When Coleman was a toddler, Jason took Coleman shopping at the grocery store down the road from our house.

Coleman couldn't buckle himself into his car seat or unbuckle himself to get out. Jason couldn't do it either. This little difficulty never stopped Jason. I buckled Coleman in his seat at home, then Jason would drive to the store, ride down the ramp of his handicap-accessible van, and watch for a nice person to walk by.

When he found someone who looked friendly, he'd stop them in the parking lot.
"Excuse me, ma'am, could you help me get my son out of his car seat?"
Jason usually got great results this way.
How many people would say no to a guy in a wheelchair?

Coleman would ride into the store on Jason's lap and then climb into the shopping cart. By hooking his arm in the basket of the shopping cart, Jason could pull the cart with him as he drove his wheelchair down the aisles. Coleman sat in the cart and grabbed needed items off the shelves.

If an item was out of Coleman's reach, Jason would ask another shopper for help. "Excuse me, ma'am, would you help us get that peanut butter?"

Once Jason paid for the groceries, he found another kind shopper to help him load the bags and Coleman into the van. Jason was always able to find someone more than willing to take time out of his or her own shopping trip to buckle Coleman in his car seat.

Coleman got used to asking for help.
It didn't matter where we went, if we needed something, Coleman said, "We'll just ask a ma'am to help us." Male or female, to Coleman, someone who was willing to lend a hand was called a "ma'am."

As years passed, Jason and I got better at "asking a ma'am" to help us too.
We got better at letting people serve us, help us, care for us, love us.

People who left two hundred meals in my Winder Dairy box.
People in high school who were friends before Jason broke his neck and friends after.
The neighbor who fixed our leaky refrigerator.
Random guys who lifted his wheelchair out of uneven terrain or pushed him through wet grass on the lacrosse field.
Friends who bottled my peaches because it was all I could eat when I was sick.
Nurses who stayed late to talk because they wanted to get to know Jason better.
Neighbors who helped me carry his chair up the stairs when our elevator broke.
Endless people who picked up things he dropped, grabbed stuff out of his bag, put things away for him, helped him get his food, set up ramps for him, and made his life happen.

And Patti at J&J Nursery, who called to tell Jason where to find the Sunsweets.

Hundreds of individuals have served us over the years.
People who gave us the Slurpees called compassion, kindness, time, and help.

I think of them, and those familiar feelings of intense gratitude come rushing back to me.

I can still see their Slurpee Service. I can still feel their Slurpee Love. Different flavors, same sweetness.

And we love them back. Fiercely. Intensely. Loyally.

Service does that. We decide to be a little vulnerable and let people in. They help us with something we need. Then our hearts overflow with love for them.

That's quite a trade-off for letting go of some independence.

JASON

The year I broke my neck, the Boston Celtics beat the Houston Rockets and won the NBA Championship. I was a Celtics fan, and those were the days of the great Larry Bird. But the Celtics player I loved the most was Danny Ainge, former BYU basketball star.

One afternoon, I was lying in bed when out of the blue I received a phone call. To my utter astonishment, it was Danny Ainge. He had heard about me and my accident and called to give me encouragement. We spent a few minutes talking. He said, "If you're ever in Boston, I'll get you tickets to a game."

Dad is a good sport and a huge fan of supporting me in the things I love. Along with two of my friends, Dad and I flew from Boise, Idaho to Boston, Massachusetts to see a game in the Boston Garden. I was in basketball heaven! The banners, the retired numbers hung in the rafters, and watching Danny and Larry Bird play on the signature parquet floor was like living a dream.

Danny told me to meet him after the game outside the Celtics' locker room. We gathered in the hallway and visited with Danny for a few minutes. Suddenly, Danny glanced up and called out to someone who had just left the opposing team's locker room. "Hey, Michael! I have somebody I want you to meet."

We turned to see who he was talking to and there he was. Michael Jordan. I couldn't believe it. The Celtics had played the Chicago Bulls that night, and we had seen Michael work his magic on the court. And now he talking to us, three starstruck kids from Boise, Idaho. Michael and Danny spent about fifteen minutes with us in that hallway in the Boston Garden. Danny probably didn't think it was that big of a deal to make a phone call to a fifteen-year-old kid who had just broken his neck or to offer tickets to one of his games or to introduce us to a fellow basketball player.

But I will never forget his kindness. And neither will my dad. Kindness isn't a big thing. It's a lot of little things, and those little things make all the difference.

FACEBOOK POST – JANUARY 17, 2020 (DAY 238)

Processing information is hard for me now.
Instructions.
Problem solving.
Tasks.

It's all difficult.
My brain is slower. I'm forgetful.
If it requires me to make sense of instructions, I feel my mind rejecting anything beyond the first few sentences.
I'm not really worried about it – it's part of grieving and will probably get better with some more time.

I lost my pancreas nine years ago.
I am now a pseudo-diabetic and insulin dependent.

A few months ago my insulin pump's warranty expired, the company was discontinuing the production of new ones, and my supplies were running out.
I had to get a new pump.

But I couldn't even click on the manufacturer's website, much less figure out how to apply for a new one.
My nemesis, those pesky instructions on how to get the job done, loomed large.

I saw my friend at church.
She's a diabetic, and so is her daughter. They already had the new pump.

"I'm having a hard time figuring out what to do," I said.
She didn't hesitate to reply, "I'll help you."

It was one of those moments though.
A moment when, for a couple of seconds, I could feel my self-talk pulling on me:
"I should be able to do it myself.
It should be so easy to figure out.
Just do it yourself, Kolette."

Then I got real.
Who was I kidding??!!
This was totally hard for me to figure out!
I said, "Yes, I'd love the help."

She sent me a little list of things to do.
Offered to help me fill out the paperwork.

My pump arrived in the mail.
I bypassed the instruction sheet and headed to Brooke's house.
She got my pump set up.
And taught me how to refill the cartridge.

I went back a few days later to refill it again.
I needed double the lessons.
She gave me a card with super simple steps for how to refill it at home.
Three days later I pulled out the card and did it myself.
And again three days after that.

I don't need that card anymore.
I can refill my cartridge on my own.

I tuned into a Facebook event yesterday from the company that makes my pump. They have received FDA approval for a new system. As I listened I kept thinking, "Brooke will tell me what this is all about."
She reads the instructions for me.
Because right now I have a hard time doing it myself.

Thanks, Brooke.
For offering exactly what I actually need.
It's a bigger deal than you think it is, girl.

CHAPTER 7
WE CONQUER SOME THRESHOLDS

I've spent the week sitting in the same spot on the Oregon Coast where this picture was taken two years ago.

I love this pic! It captures Jason's smile perfectly.

This trip has been a lot like the Hall family reunion last month at Deer Valley where Jason was around every corner.
Except missing.

Missing the "Hall Anything Goes" games.
Missing the t-shirts and swim day and ordering Shirley Temples.
Missing the whole family being together.
Giving wheelchair rides to thirteen nieces and nephews.
Missing the same childhood stories told a thousand times already.
They were still told, but Jason's version was just...
Missing.

Then this week in Oregon with my family.
Missing the donut run to the bakery each morning.
Missing the blue skies.
The sunshine.
The sound of the waves and salty air settling on our skin.
Missing walking into town for ice cream at night.

Missing watching the kids build an epic sand castle.
Missing the salt-water taffy 5,348 flavor tasting.
Missing the Walla Walla sweet onion rings in season at Burgerville.
Missing.

At night during the Hall reunion, I hid out in my room.
I got tired faster than normal.
I cried when I said my prayers.
Then read my book for a while.
Finally I ventured out to where the ultimate family Uno game
was underway.

That was a month ago.
I did it again last night here in Oregon.
Walked in to grab warmer clothes to sit by the beach fire.
I never left my room.
Read my book instead.

Jason's family just let me be.
My family just let me be.
I just let myself be.

I love being here with five out of six siblings.
Those times are rare as we get older.
The beach is healing and calming and super fun.
A blast, really!
But today I'm missing what's missing.

JASON

At first, I didn't have a power wheelchair, just a manual one. I wasn't strong enough to push that chair on any surface that had any kind of a texture. If you put me on grass or carpet, I couldn't push very far. If you put me on hardwood or tile or linoleum, that was my turf. I owned linoleum.

My parents converted a closet into a handicap-accessible bathroom for me. When I first saw the finished bathroom, my heart filled with joy—wall-to-wall linoleum joy. There was linoleum as far as the eye could see.

I cruised over to the shower to see if I could fit, then under the sink, and over to the toilet. I could roll all over that bathroom by myself. When you can't push yourself around and then suddenly you're in a place where you can, it's like being let loose on the last day of school. Sheer bliss. That's what it was like to be in my new bathroom.

When I'd finished inspecting the space, Dad went out the door, and I followed in my chair, so excited to be pushing myself. I got to the doorway and BAM! I was stopped. I looked down to see what brick wall or large boulder was blocking my forward progress. All I saw was a little gold threshold, the metal piece they put between carpet and linoleum to divide a room. It was maybe a couple of centimeters high. That was what had stopped my forward progression. It was pretty much a blow to my masculinity.

My dad, who loves a challenge, took a twenty-dollar bill out of his pocket and placed it on the floor in front of me. I remember thinking, "Twenty bucks? I'd sell my sister for twenty bucks!" I backed up and I pushed and I worked and I pushed and I worked and I gave it everything I had in my exit from the bathroom. I hit that threshold and BAM! Again I was stopped. Dad put another twenty dollars on the ground, and I backed up. I pushed and I worked and pushed and worked, and again I couldn't clear the threshold.

I know what you're thinking. You're thinking maybe I wasn't trying so hard just to see how many twenties Dad would lay down before I rolled over that threshold. But that's not how it was. I was giving it everything I had. Soon there were five twenty-dollar bills on the floor.

As the twenties piled up, my attempts got weaker. Dad knew I was going to lose this battle in my war, and he knew, as I do now, that it's ok to lose a battle as long as you don't give up the fight. Dad put the money back in his pocket and wrapped his arm around me. "Keep trying," he said.

I thought, "Dad, what about good sportsmanship? Throw me a fiver." But the money was long gone, and in the end, the two words he left me were worth a mountain of twenties. *Keep trying.*

Keep trying.

Every day for the next month, I asked one of my siblings to push me into that bathroom. Every day I pushed and I worked and pushed and worked to get over that threshold. I will never forget how it felt the day my front wheels rolled over that threshold and my back wheels followed. My arms went up in the air. In that little hallway in Boise, Idaho, I had overcome.

KOLETTE

There were many thresholds blocking our path over the years.

When we went to Oregon without Jason six weeks after he died, I constantly felt like something was missing. The one who had always been with me wasn't there anymore. Every memory contained a hole the size and shape of Jason.

I was missing what was missing.

Just like Jason in that handicap-accessible bathroom, my husband is gone and I am facing another little gold threshold, and I'm not quite sure if I'm strong enough to conquer it.

I waited three weeks to have Jason's funeral.

My parents and brother's family went to Yosemite National Park in California the week after Jason died.
Coleman was already scheduled to go with them.
I didn't want Coleman to miss that trip.
I tagged along instead.
Ten days after Jason passed away, Coleman and I were in Yosemite.

We scheduled the funeral for the Saturday after we returned home.
It gave us some time.
Time for Jason's brothers and their families to come from Connecticut.
Time to plan things the way I wanted them.
Time to think about what to say at the funeral.
Time to pause, be together, think things through, do the details without the rush.
Time to write his obituary.
Time to design his funeral program how I wanted it.
A little bit of time to feel and celebrate and remember.

The funeral home took good care of Jason over the three weeks before his service.
As a matter of fact, they told me that more and more people are waiting.
It's actually not as crazy as it seemed at first.

I loved that Jason lingered during that time. That's probably my favorite reason of all for waiting.

Our trip to Yosemite was a balm.
Gorgeous hikes to powerful waterfalls were healing. The Yosemite Valley is picturesque and almost heavenly as the sheer cliffs rise up from the meadow.
I felt peace there.
I felt love there.
I felt light there.

And every handicap sign with the stick figure wheelchair guy made me think of Jason. I saw him everywhere.

We drove four hours from Yosemite to spend our last two days in Sequoia and Kings Canyon National Parks. When we arrived at our hotel, Coleman opened up his backpack and pulled out his blanket then started digging for his all-time favorite stuffed animal, the first Beanie Boo he ever got, Turtle.

Turtle was loved.
He was worn.
He was one of about thirty Beanie Boos that live in Coleman's room.
But Turtle was his favorite.

And Turtle was gone.
We looked everywhere. In the suitcase, in the backpack, in the hotel room, under the beds, in the drawers, in every car of our caravan.
We said a prayer. "Heavenly Father, please help us know where to look for Turtle."

Coleman went to look in another room, and I cried.
I cried hard.
I cried harder than I had cried in the two weeks since Jason had died.
In discouragement and defeat, I thought, "It's bad enough that Coleman had to lose his dad. Does he have to lose Turtle too?"
I knelt on the floor and pleaded, "Please. Help us find Turtle."

We didn't find him.
As we drove to the airport, I felt the loss of Turtle sink into my chest, and I just wanted to fill the empty space.
I immediately went to eBay to search for the exact replica of Turtle.
This is it! This is the same one! Same flippers. Same smile. Same non-droopy eyes.

We bought it to replace the Turtle he loved.
It arrived a week later.
But it wasn't exactly right. The cheeks weren't exactly the same.
The worn spots weren't there. The love wasn't there.
It wasn't Turtle.
I went into the bathroom and cried again.

Turtle is missing. Just like Jason.
And replacements are just not the same.

Coleman is good at talking to Alexa. She seems to listen to him better than Jason or me.
"Alexa, play "Sunflower" by Post Malone."
"Alexa, tell me a joke."
"Alexa, what's the score of the Cowboys game?"

I think it would be nice if I could just ask Alexa to help me with what I really need.
"Alexa, find Turtle."
"Alexa, help me feel Jason with me all the time."
"Alexa, tell me how to get over this threshold."
"Alexa, make it better."

Sometimes I just don't feel strong enough to conquer a life without Jason.
I'm not exactly sure if I can do it.

When Coleman was a year old, I decided to run the Ogden half marathon. I ran track in junior high, but I don't love running distances. My neighborhood is full of runners, so I jumped on the 13.1-mile bandwagon and decided to go for it.

I researched a training schedule for beginners.
I did my runs during Coleman's naps so Jason could watch over him while I was gone.
One mile. Two miles. Three miles. Four miles. Five miles.

Then I got stuck. I couldn't make it past five miles without feeling like I was going to hyperventilate, barely stumbling into the house to lie on the floor and recover.

Mile one through four seemed to get easier and easier but as soon as I got to mile five, I felt like I could hardly pick my feet up to move forward.

It was around this time of the summer when we had our yearly Hall family reunion with Jason's family. We traveled up the mountain to Park City, Utah to stay for a week with his parents and all of the cousins. I mapped out a running route. I only had time that day to do three miles so I opted for the loop that went up and down hills around Jason's parents' home. I did that three-mile loop multiple times that week.

The reunion ended, and we traveled the hour back down the mountain to our home.
I did my run the next day.
One mile. Two miles. Three miles. Four miles. Five miles. Six miles. Seven miles.

I could hardly believe it! I did seven miles without feeling like I was going to pass out. I felt lighter, more agile, faster.

The elevation in Park City is close to 7,000 feet. I ran up hills and down. The route was harder than what I had been running at home. When I returned to our hometown elevation of 4,285 feet, my body could feel the difference. It had a change of scenery and a new point of view and had done something harder than what I was doing at home.

That five-mile barrier became a thing of the past. It was the doing something hard that made me strong enough to conquer what was holding me back.

JASON

I had always wanted to attend Brigham Young University, so when I started there as a freshman, I was living my dream. It was the first time I lived away from home after breaking my neck. My parents had always taken care of me, and at BYU I had a roommate they paid to lay me down at night and fix my meals. I had an aide who came in every day to get me up. The aide was my cousin's husband, but I had never met him until I got to BYU. I didn't know what to expect, and I was scared.

What if the aide didn't come one day and just left me in bed? What if my roommate and I had a fight, and he didn't come home to help me? Would I have to sleep in my chair? This was my chance to live my dream, but when my chance arrived, I wasn't sure if I could actually do it. The only accessible housing on campus in 1989 was a married student apartment that had been converted for me. There were no other freshmen besides my roommate living nearby. Having caregivers who weren't my parents was terrifying. I was lonely. I wasn't sure if I was strong enough to overcome the fear I felt. I wasn't sure if I could overcome the loneliness or if I could find my place at BYU.

At BYU there is the huge block Y on the mountainside above campus. It is larger than the letters of the Hollywood sign in Los Angeles. That Y was on the mountain directly above my apartment. One day after my roommate had been asked out on yet another date, I was driving my wheelchair home feeling sorry for myself. I looked up at the mountain and thought, "That's a good question. Why am I here? Why aren't I home?"

I was discouraged and alone, facing another threshold that I wasn't sure I could push over, and no amount of twenty-dollar bills was going to motivate me.

I called my parents and told them I was scared and lonely and that things were really, really hard. "Jason, you can always come home," Dad said. I fell silent. I knew that if I opened my mouth, I would tell him I was quitting.

I hung up the phone and closed my eyes. My high school achievements had earned me the right to many college scholarships, but I had only sent my standardized test scores to two schools: BYU and Boston College. I only looked at Boston College because my sports hero, Danny Ainge, played for the Boston Celtics at the time. BYU had always been my first choice, really the only choice. I thought about going home—really thought about it. If I went home, it was likely I would never leave Boise again, never get a college education, never achieve any of my dreams. My life would be easier, but I couldn't imagine it would be better.

With my last speck of determination, I decided to stay. Nine times that semester, I made the six-hour drive to Boise, but I always came back to Provo. I sailed through the year with a 4.0 GPA because I spent all my time in the library studying.

Then my mom did something that helped push me over the threshold. She bought my roommate and me meal passes to the dorm cafeteria. We ate there every day. Not only was this a good thing because my roommate couldn't cook, but it forced me to be around other freshmen. I got out of my apartment and started to make friends. Someone invited me to get involved in student government. I helped plan a pep rally and found purpose in serving others.

Little by little, I found my place. I became stronger.

My decision to stay at BYU was a defining moment in my life. If I had gone home, I would have missed out on dances and running into friends on campus and getting ice cream at the Creamery. I never would have had the professor who made us practice grammar rules on romance novel excerpts. I would have missed out on speaking to the entire student body as their president. I wouldn't have bought the season football tickets we still use almost thirty years later. I would have missed out on falling in love with Kolette.

I would have missed out on all the things that were waiting on the other side of that threshold.

When I broke my neck, I spent three weeks in a hospital in Grand Junction, Colorado. A few days after the accident, I received a package filled with posters and cards from friends and family. My parents hung the posters all over my room so that wherever I looked I was reminded of my friends' support. My friends also included a cassette tape in that package. While I was in surgery, my friends had gotten together and recorded an hour of jokes and encouragement and laughter on that cassette. I listened to that tape so often the tape broke. My parents taped it back together, and I listened again.

When I was moved to the University of Utah hospital in Salt Lake City, my friends drove six hours from Boise to visit me. Jonah was one of my best friends even though we were as different as night and day. I was straight-laced sports fanatic, and he was a laid back, free-spirited musician. I came from a devout religious family, and he doubted the existence of God.

One by one, my friends entered my hospital room. Just seeing their faces lifted my spirits. Jonah was the last to come in. He took a few steps into my room, and all the color left his face. "Hi Jason, how are ya...?" he said and passed out before he could finish his sentence.

The last time he had seen me, I was standing six feet tall, 175 pounds, strong and fit. When he saw me in the hospital, I was weak and sickly, unable to stand, weighing 118 pounds. You could literally see every bone in my body under my skin. I had tubes sticking out of my arms and legs and the markings of a recently-removed halo brace on my head. All this, accompanied by the stifling smell of the hospital, put Jonah over the edge.

A nurse helped Jonah up, took him out of the room, and found him a place to lie down until he felt well enough to come back. On Jonah's second try, he came into my room, took a few steps toward my bed, and said, "Hi Jason, how are ya...?" and passed out again.

The nurses came back. They helped Jonah to another room to lie down. Thirty minutes later he was ready to make another attempt. All conversation stopped when he walked in my room. All eyes were on Jonah. The nurses followed him in, arms outstretched behind him in the ready position. "Hi Jason, how are ya...?" Jonah passed out again! He hadn't even said a complete sentence.

Eventually Jonah was able to stay upright when he came into my room. I'm sure fainting was embarrassing and painful for him. Who wants to fall three times onto a hard tile floor in front of your friends? But Jonah kept coming back. No one would have faulted him if he had just waited in a different room until the visit was over. No one would have criticized him if he hadn't wanted to come back again.

But he did come back. Our friendship mattered more to him than the embarrassment and pain. He kept trying, and eventually he made it through that door and into the room. Jonah conquered his threshold because he was my friend.

KOLETTE

Two weeks before I was supposed to run that half marathon, a searing, blinding pain shot up my chest and over my shoulder. I fell to my knees and almost passed out on our bedroom floor.

Coleman was fifteen months old. Our friend watched him while Jason and my sister rushed me to the hospital. A gallstone had gotten stuck in the duct of my pancreas, and my pancreas was digesting itself. Gallstone pancreatitis.

The pancreas doesn't like to be messed with.
When you do mess with it, the pain is overwhelming.

I was immediately admitted to the hospital.
That first week I gained sixty pounds in fluid.
I couldn't digest regular food so they gave me a TPN (Total Parenteral Nutrition) to bypass my gastrointestinal tract. They inserted a tube into my vein then mixed up a concoction of nutrients, put them in an IV-type bag, and sent the nutrients into my body through a tube.
I carried around a bagful of liquid nutrients for seven months.

While I was in the hospital, my organs began shutting down.
One morning, a CNA came in to check my vitals and saw I wasn't responding.
She saved my life.

I was in the ICU for two weeks and then went to a pancreas specialist at the University of Utah Huntsman Cancer Center. I didn't have cancer, but this was the doctor to see for complicated pancreas issues. Before my appointment, the doctor caught a glimpse of me and told her residents, "Wow, there's a pregnant woman out there on a TPN. That is tough."

I wasn't pregnant, I just looked it because of the fluid that had collected in my body.

She was an incredible doctor.
The one who handled the tricky cases. The tough problems.
She removed my gallbladder and seventy percent of my pancreas.
She attached a pseudocyst to my stomach to drain fluid so it wouldn't continue to collect in my abdomen.
My abdominal muscles were shredded from the excess fluid, so she rebuilt my abdominal wall and gave me a new belly button.

I was left with a six-inch scar running down my stomach. I am now insulin dependent and use an insulin pump. I'm not exactly Type I diabetic and not exactly Type II diabetic. My diabetes is trauma induced. I'm Type Me diabetic.

During the two years of illness and recovery, I missed some things. A lot of things.

Coleman was too young for Jason to care for full time and I was too sick, so my brother and sister-in-law traded back and forth with Jason's mom to take care of Coleman. The pain was so severe I couldn't have our wiggly fifteen-month-old near me for more than a few minutes at a time.

I missed Coleman.

I spent hours on the sofa with my purple G2 drink and my TPN backpack, breathing shallow breaths because anything else hurt too much. Much of my hair fell out. My skin peeled from the palms of my hands and the bottom of my feet. My teeth deteriorated. I missed the taste of real food.

My stamina and energy plummeted. Each day I walked three houses down the street to the mailbox and back. Then I took a nap. I missed having a body that could train for a half marathon. I missed pain-free days.

I no longer had the strength to roll Jason over during the night to prevent pressure sores. I couldn't cook meals or help Jason throughout the day. We hired Jason's cousin to be our first ever 24/7 live-in medical aide.

I missed regular family life.

My sister dropped everything and cared for me at home. Neighbors took me to doctor appointments, iron infusion sessions, physical therapy. Friends sat with me even when I fell asleep in the middle of the visit. I missed being able to do more than just breathe and sleep.

I missed what was missing.

I suppose that's true for a lot of things in life.
The moments when I'm looking for something more.
The lost chances.
The opportunities not taken.
The holes left from broken relationships.
The sorrow from disappointments.
The pain, the loneliness, the discouragement, the struggle.
The times when I'm just missing something important.

I imagine Jason in that bathroom in Boise. His injury never allowed him to push his wheelchair with much force. It's why he used a power chair. But I can see him in his manual chair. I can see him press the heels of his hands on the wheels because he couldn't move his fingers to grip. I can see him lean over and slowly push. He probably grunted a little, took a deep breath, and gritted his teeth.

He was stopped. And stopped again. And then again.
The ability to use his legs was missing. Use of his hands was missing. Life as he knew it was missing.
But he kept pushing. He kept his chair moving forward until he slowly rolled over that threshold to the other side.

I miss the things that are missing.
I can't replace the irreplaceable.
These wounds might never heal completely.
My scar might never fade.
The holes left from things that are missing might never be filled.

But the wounds and scars and holes from missing pieces are now part of me. Signs that I did something hard, that I'm still doing hard things.
Evidence that I'm leaning in, taking a deep breath, gritting my teeth, and slowly pushing over yet another threshold.

In spite of what's missing.

FACEBOOK POST - OCTOBER 13, 2019 (DAY 143)

We went to General Conference, a worldwide broadcast for our church.
One of the speakers talked about our family in a message called "Fruit."
I got to choose the photos he shared. (Thank goodness!)
He referenced Coleman's funeral talk.

He repeated the phrase Jason told Coleman every night since the day he was born.
"Dad loves you, Heavenly Father loves you, and you're a good boy."

My breath caught for just a moment.
I haven't heard those words for 143 days.

I was fine at the Conference Center.
Filled with love and joy and happiness that millions more people have the chance to know Jason because of our story told there.

As we went to bed that night, Coleman started to cry.
He doesn't do that often.
"I just miss Dad," he said as the tears flowed for both of us.
"I do too. Let's cry together," I said.
After that, it was a hard few days for me. I kept thinking of those words they told each other each day. As Coleman grew older, it became a game to see who could say it first.

Coleman would burst into our room in the mornings and call out as quickly as he could, "Coleman loves you, Heavenly Father loves you, and you're a good boy, counts as night time!!" Jason would try to beat him to it, and if he was too late, he would groan, "Awww, you got me!"

I feel like I am a good mom, and I'm doing this single mother thing pretty well.

But there are things I cannot replace.
There are things that will always be missing.
There are things I cannot fix.

I tried saying the words to Coleman after Jason died, but it felt strange and not right.
It was their thing.
Their ritual.
Their tradition.
Like watching Cowboys games together, cheering side-by-side in the family room.
It was between father and son.

There are things I can't replace.

This week I am mourning the loss of twelve words that I will never hear again between the boys I love.
Missing what's missing.

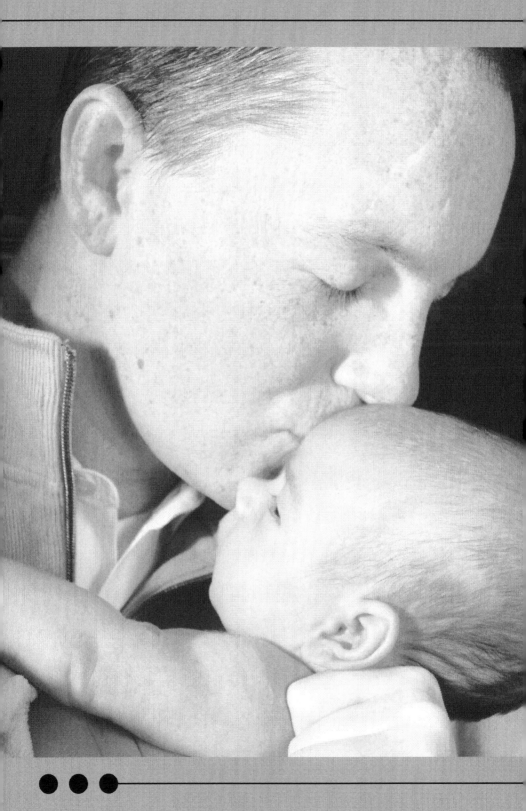

CHAPTER 8
WE RIDE THE ELEVATOR ONE LAST TIME

FACEBOOK POST – JUNE 25, 2019 (DAY 32)

I spy with my little eye...
3 wheelchairs.
1 hand bike.
4 pressure-regulating seat cushions.
1 charger and a spare for travel.
1 charger with an international plug.
3 neck braces from the Avengers wreck.
A giant Ziploc bag of specialty gear.
A pair of foot stabilizing boots.
A bunch of adaptive writing tools.
1 boxful of medical supplies.

Jason took none of this with him.
I've decided that I don't need to keep it either.

It represents the burden.
The struggle.
The hard stuff.
The daily pain.
The challenge to overcome.

I'm ok letting it go.
He's free of it, and I can be too.

Good riddance, actually.
See ya later, alligator.
Ciao!
Bye, Felicia!
Cya.
Don't let the door hit ya on the way out.
Hasta la vista, baby.

It's all going to a good home. My sister helped me create the pile. Every nook and cranny of the house has been de-medicalized.

My sister-in-law arranged for an organization to pick it all up this morning to donate to people who can really use it. They'll take it all. I love that.

Here's to letting go of the stuff weighing us down. Even the tools that used to help but don't anymore.

Let it go, girl.
My pleasure.

UPDATE: I had a 15-second cry while sitting on the steps in our garage after I saw that the pile was actually gone.
I'm a short crier.
These things were so much a part of Jason's independence. His life. But then I remembered he doesn't need it anymore, so I can move on from it too.
I'm still good with letting the stuff go.

KOLETTE

Jason gave a lot of talks to youth groups and companies and corporations. He'd often end with, "I know that there will come a day when I will stand from my wheelchair, hold it high above my head, throw it as far as I can, and run until I drop."

We both believed it would happen.

What neither of us really thought about is that when Jason died, the standing from his chair definitely happened. And probably the running till he dropped.

But his wheelchair didn't go with him. It stayed here with me. It was too heavy to hold high above my head and throw as far as I could.
So instead, I donated it to someone who could use it.

When Jason and I lived in Connecticut, some friends invited us to the Poconos for a day of boating and summer fun. On the drive over, Jason said, "I don't want to go in the boat," meaning, "Don't suggest that I go in the boat in front of people who will insist that I go in the boat." Got it.

We arrived at the lake, and I went into the house to help with lunch preparations. Jason headed down to the dock in his wheelchair. About three minutes later, one of the kids came running to the house. "Jason is getting in the boat!"

I guess he changed his mind.

I walked down to the dock to see if they needed any help and immediately assessed the situation from a distance. There was Jason, sitting in the back of the boat. Four big guys had lifted him in and were adjusting and arranging him from their positions on the dock so he'd be steady and safe.

All of their weight was on the boat side of the dock.
The boat side of the dock tipped toward the water at a precarious angle.

I felt like I was running in slow motion as I took off toward the water, arms outstretched and pointing, yelling as loud as I could to alert anyone within proximity, "The chaaiiiirrrrr!"

Jason's $15,000 wheelchair was also on the boat side of the dock. It also tipped at a precarious angle.

The men had lifted Jason safely into the boat, but his chair was poised to fall into the water at any moment.

By paying attention to Jason, everyone had missed the other vital thing sitting on the dock.

Jason's chair did not fall into the water, but I nearly had a heart attack wondering if it would.

JASON

After breaking my neck, of all the countless things I had to learn to do again, keeping my balance was far and away the most difficult. From the moment I was off the respirator and healthy enough to be out of bed, my therapists worked every day to help me regain my balance while sitting up. This may not seem like a difficult thing to do, but without the assistance of my abdominal muscles to keep me upright or the help of my trunk muscles to keep me steady, maintaining my balance took some serious work.

From my first day in a wheelchair, I had a Velcro strap that went around my chest and the back of my wheelchair to keep me from falling to the ground. At first, I leaned on my strap all of the time, but after a while I got strong enough that I relied on it less and less often. By the time I left the hospital, I had gotten to the point where I was fairly secure in my balance. Still, the ground looked pretty ominous and wanting to keep my face as far as I could from the concrete, I decided to keep the strap.

Months later, my mom was in my room helping me get ready for church. It felt like a regular Sunday. Little did I know that this particular Sunday, my mom was plotting against me.

Everything was going normally. My mom helped me put on my pants, sat me in my chair, buttoned up my white shirt, tied my tie, and slid my sport coat on. Then, acting as though it was something we did every day, she removed my strap.

I proceeded to inform her that this was not going to work. I tried to explain that I needed the strap and without it, I would fall out of my chair. The idea horrified me, but clearly, it didn't horrify her.

She told me that while I was in the hospital, one of the therapists told her I could get to a point where I would no longer need the strap to keep my balance. My mom informed me that I had, in fact, reached that point whether I knew it or not. She said that she believed in me and was sure I'd be just fine without it.

I, on the other hand, was positive she was wrong. It wasn't written on the calendar, and I hadn't heard a magic bell ring. How could anyone know for sure I'd reached the point of no strap? But the strap was gone, and it was obvious I was going to church strapless unless I could convince one of my siblings to disobey Mom's edict. I was pretty sure that wasn't going to happen.

I was furious. How could she do this to me? Did she want me to fall? They loaded me in the car, and we headed to church. Glaring at my mom throughout the entire service, I concentrated on sitting up. As I worked to keep myself upright, I silently waited for the moment when my efforts would fail and I would fall. Then I could prove to my mother I was right and she was wrong.

Contrary to my expectations, I sat up through the entire meeting. I was suddenly quite frightened. This was a big problem. If my mom saw that I could sit up without my strap, I would definitely never see it again. The services ended, and my mother pushed me out the chapel doors. It was then or never. I spied a crack in the sidewalk and seized my chance. My front wheels hit the crack, and as the chair bounced just a bit, I threw myself out of my chair. My upper body slammed against the concrete, pinning my legs underneath my torso. My mother came from behind my chair to help me get off the ground. "See?" I said. "I was right. I told you I need my strap!"

Once I was safely back in my chair, my mom gave me one of her I'm-too-smart-for-you smiles. "You may fall a few times, but eventually you'll figure it out." I fumed. My strap was gone, and the only thing I was going to get from falling out of my chair on purpose was a concussion.

My mom knew it was important for me to learn balance. I sit up today in my wheelchair without a cumbersome strap because my mom was willing to let me fall. Now that I'm a parent, I can understand how difficult it must have been to remove my strap. My mom never took the easy way out, especially when she knew her actions would help me in the long run.

Sometimes all we need to create balance in our own lives is to remove the restraints and crutches we think are keeping us steady. They're often only holding us back.

KOLETTE

I was a school tutor while we lived in Connecticut, helping kids with homework and teaching them study and writing skills. One family I worked for, the Checketts, consisted of three boys and one girl who ranged in age from elementary to high school. Having four brothers of my own, I was used to dealing with the shenanigans of boys.

One day while I was there, the Checketts boys were practicing on their balance board, which is a rectangular board similar in shape to a skateboard that sits on top of a wood and metal cylinder. They used this balance board to hone their snowboarding and skateboarding skills.

"Kolette, come try the balance board," they coaxed.
Of course I was going to try it. It didn't scare me.

Not getting any instruction or asking any useful questions, I set one end of the board on the ground, put my foot on it, then set my other foot on the raised end of the board. One second later, the cylinder spun out from under the board and spun me with it, catapulting me into the air like a cartoon character. I landed flat on the floor. The boys ended up on the floor with me as they erupted in hysterical laughter.

Clearly, I had failed the balance board.

Balance is a tricky thing. It sometimes looks easier to achieve than it is.

To achieve balance on the dock in the Poconos, a few people standing on the other side of the dock would have created a more even distribution of weight while the men lifted Jason into the boat.

Achieving balance on the balance board required a constant shifting of weight from one side to the other, anticipating and sensing what direction the cylinder was rotating and adjusting my weight with it.

Achieving balance in my life is kind of similar.
Sometimes I pay more attention to one area of my life.
Sometimes it's because I have to. Sometimes it's a choice.
Usually I am most steady when I make small adjustments, focusing on what needs my attention the most at a given time.

I create computer-generated designs for personal die-cutting machines. Because the holiday season is my most profitable time of the year, from October through December I am focused on work. I do that on purpose. Then January comes, and I take a break. Work is no longer a priority. That's on purpose, too.

To me, that's balance.
Evaluating what I need to focus on in the moment is balance.
Being okay with changes in my priorities is balance.
Letting go of things that may not be of immediate importance is balance.

A few years after we were married, Jason had a speaking engagement in England, and we stopped in Holland on the way there. His mother and grandparents immigrated to the United States from the Netherlands when his mom was just three years old. We were headed to see the town where she was born, the places we had heard stories about, and the family we had only met through photographs and their occasional visits to the States.

For many years I acted as Jason's medical aide when we traveled. That changed later in our married life, but it was just Jason and me for our trip to Holland. Neither of us had traveled very much, especially with a wheelchair, and not knowing what to expect, we took all the things we used at home for Jason's care.

We had Jason's power wheelchair complete with a power converter to charge the batteries each night.
We had his manual wheelchair because there were no handicap rental vans available in Holland.
We brought his shower chair that could roll into the shower and get wet.
We lugged along two large suitcases, a carry-on, and the backpack that hung on Jason's chair.

We arranged to stay in a hotel in Amsterdam that we thought was located directly across from the airport. After a wild time at baggage claim, I placed one suitcase and the carry-on bag on top of the shower chair so I could push it with one hand. With the other hand, I pushed Jason's folded manual chair. Fortunately, his backpack hung on the back of his power chair.

We manhandled our load out of the airport. "Thank goodness our hotel is just across the street," I thought. Ha. Ha. We stood outside and faced a complex network of roads "across the street" from the airport. Since this was before Siri could help us with directions, we had to find our own way to the hotel.

We tried one street. It was wrong.
We backtracked and tried another. Still not right.
I was hanging in there with my awkward load until we hit the cobblestones.
Wheelchairs and cobblestones don't mix.
Frustrated, sweaty, and a little angry, I told Jason I was going to park myself and all of our stuff on the corner while he figured out where we were supposed to go.

An hour later, we finally made it to the hotel and checked in.
That night, after an evening exploring Amsterdam, we blew the power on our whole floor because our converter couldn't handle the wheelchair charger.
That meant Jason's chair was not charged overnight.

The next morning, we hauled all our stuff to the train station for a short ride to meet our family in Utrecht. When we arrived at the Utrecht station, Jason's chair batteries were blinking close to empty. I pushed the shower chair, suitcases, backpack, and manual chair off the train then went back for Jason. We had to make it about two hundred yards to the next hotel to meet his Dutch aunts and uncles.

I pushed our gear to the hotel and found a spot to park it.
I pushed Jason to the hotel.
When we rolled into the lobby, he had no juice left. And neither did I.

We now had a shower chair, a manual chair, and a dead 350-pound power chair that had to be pushed from one destination to the next.

Jason's family came to the rescue. They found a hospital that had its own generator and a willing electrician who hooked up Jason's chair to some jumper cables and charged the batteries for us. It was enough charge to get us home when the time came. We stored our power wheelchair, the shower chair, and our suitcases at the hotel until we returned to the States. Willing uncles lifted Jason in and out of cars so he could travel to every location he wanted to see in his mother's hometown.

We had a great time in Holland.
We eventually made it home, happy about the memories we made but exhausted from hauling all our stuff around.
We vowed never to travel with all of that baggage again.

Never again did the shower chair travel with us. We made do with bed baths.
Rarely did we take his manual chair. We found medical transport services that could drive us until handicap rental vans became more common.
I started taking just a carry-on when possible.
We ditched things like extra shoes and extra pants and wore the same clothes over and over again.

Some things were vital, others we left home.
Medical supplies beat out the extra shirts.
The right power adapter let us charge his wheelchair in foreign countries.
We learned to let go of the things that didn't matter as much.
Without so much baggage, our journeys became lighter.

It affected how we worked together, how we solved problems, and most importantly, how we felt about traveling together. Carrying a lighter load helped us enjoy our trips and each other more.

Creating balance in my life often means I have to let go the stuff weighing me down.
The stuff that makes it hard to get across the cobblestones.
The stuff that seems necessary but ends up just being baggage.

In our most recent home, we had an elevator. A full-fledged, push-the-button-to-open-the-automatic-door kind of elevator. Jason used it every day to get to the basement. It was one of our best life tools.

Jason and I got stuck in the elevator once.
We had to wait until the repairman could get us out.
After that, I only used it to transport the Christmas decorations from one floor to another.

When Jason died, I decided to turn the elevator into a pantry.
My previous pantry was about two feet by two feet, located next to the elevator shaft. A coat closet took up the rest of one wall behind the elevator.
I hired someone to gut the tiny pantry, the elevator, and coat closet to make room for a large walk-in pantry.

The day the workers took out the elevator, my heart lurched just a bit.
This was Jason's, an amazing tool that served him every day.
I was so grateful we had the resources to build it into our home.
I loved it for what it was for Jason.

My heart wanted to leave it just like it was.
But it didn't serve me at all.
It was a liability when children came over and played with the buttons.

It took up space in the area where I needed space the most.

Right before they tore the elevator out, Coleman and I rode it up and down one last time, repeating the Hall family cheer over and over in honor of Jason. We recorded a video. We talked about how awesome the elevator was.
Then I let it go.

My new pantry serves me so much better than the elevator could have.

Figuring out what balance means changes with my stage of life. Sometimes finding balance means letting go of the things that aren't serving me.
Sometimes balance means hanging on with all my might to the things that matter most.

FACEBOOK POST – AUGUST 29, 2019 (DAY 97)

We've had the same BYU football season ticket seats since we were students.

Almost thirty years.

We kept them even when we lived across the country.
We kept them even when Jason was in the hospital for months.
Even when ESPN took over and we went to 8:15 pm start times.
Even when the team was wracked by injuries.
Even when we lost most games.
Even when we won.

We've watched four head coaches on the sidelines, starting with LaVell Edwards.
We were students when Ty Detmer won the Heisman.
We've seen conference championships, bowl games, and crushing upsets.

We've sung the Cougar Fight Song hundreds of times.
The Cougar mascot was our obsession. We loved watching his dance moves, his acrobatics. We relished the photo ops.
We had shirts for every game day color.
We got to the game early to see warm ups and make sure we were there for kickoff.

After Jason died, the first home game of that season was the first time in 27 years I'd been to a BYU football game without him.
That day's "first" ranks near the top of one of the hardest I think I'll face.
First game of the season.
First season without Jason.

I felt it when the season tickets Jason ordered arrived in the mail.
I felt it when I put the game schedule in my phone.
I felt it when I bought the same flag for Jason's grave that he had bought for our yard.
I felt it when I made spirit signs for his grave on rivalry game day.
I felt it when Coleman and I took a picture at the cemetery, because we always take a family picture on game day.
I felt it when I looked at Jason's last three van license plates attached to our garage wall: Cougs, Cougrs, Cougrs.

I've been feeling it for a few days.
I'm feeling it right now.

Jason is loyal.
Jason is strong.
Jason is true.
In life and as a BYU superfan.

My mom called him after every football and basketball game because she loved that he would review the highlights with her.
I'll miss that.

He and Coleman rode around the stadium scoping out the best food.
I'll miss that.

He always had to buy the new BYU hat or sweatshirt or golf shirt every season.
I'll miss that.

He knew the players to watch and what their stories were. I'm frantically looking @byufootball on Instagram and searching on Google to try to learn what he knew.
I'll miss that.

He was always optimistic about our chances for a win, even when everyone else saw no hope.
I'll miss that.

On our first game day without Jason, we went down to Provo early so we could experience it all.
My mom got our extra ticket.
I cried when the team came running out onto the field. The band played the fight song. The crowd went wild.
I missed Jason.

But I wouldn't have missed being in our spot that night.
I'm hanging on to those football tickets.

CHAPTER 9
CORN POPS BECOMES
THE BREAKFAST OF CHAMPIONS

FACEBOOK POST – JULY 13, 2019 (DAY 50)

Thirty-three years ago today, Jason broke his neck.

I wasn't on the scene till five years later, but July 13 is on my calendar because we celebrate it every year.

Every July 13, calls and texts roll in from family wishing him an enthusiastic "Happy Anniversary!"

The first year after our sister-in-law married Jason's brother, she left him a message that went something like this...

"Happy Anniversary, Jason! This seems kind of weird to celebrate, but I know it's important to you! Love you!"

Best message ever on so many levels.

Why did we celebrate the day he broke his neck?

Jason's theory was, "I can either laugh or cry, so I might as well enjoy the ride."

We usually went to a movie that day.

So this morning when Krishel suggested seeing a movie during our family getaway to Boise, I was all in.

Happy Anniversary, babe. You rocked those thirty-three years.

JASON

Potty-training is not for the faint of heart. When my brother Nathan, was about three years old, he struggled with it. My parents had gotten him through diapers and into big boy pants, and they finally felt he was making some progress.

One day Nate was out in the backyard playing with his friends, and he had to go to the bathroom. I'm sure his thought process was something like this: "If I go to the bathroom, I have to go all the way across the yard to the house, open the door, close it behind me, walk through the kitchen, and down the hall to the bathroom." That must have seemed like a lot of work so Nathan just wet his pants and continued playing with his friends. When he walked into the house later, it was obvious what he'd done. He was soaked.

Frustrated, my dad said, "Nathan, you wet your pants." Nathan looked down. "Yeah, Dad, but I didn't wet my shirt!"

Every day we get the choice. Are we going to look at the wet pants or are we going to see the dry shirt? There is a lot of both. There is a lot of sad and negative, a lot of down and depressing. But there's also a lot of happy and good and positive.

Paralysis means so much more to your body than just the inability to walk. At first, the shock is so great that essentially everything in your body shuts down. In my case, my lungs, bladder, bowels, stomach, and everything in between stopped working.

The doctors had to get involved to help my body do the work it was designed to do. Because my stomach wouldn't work properly, I needed an IV my first days in the ICU. The IV, however, was not a long-term solution. Knowing that it was going to be a long-term problem, the doctors inserted a feeding tube in my nose, down my throat, and into my stomach.

I lived for weeks on that feeding tube. Finally, to my utter excitement, the doctors decided my stomach was working again. They pulled out the tube, and I could eat real food again. Unfortunately, although my stomach had resolved its differences with my body, the muscles in my arms still weren't at optimal strength.

This meant that the nurses and aides had to feed me. There must be a "feeding patients" class in nursing school, because all my nurses and aides fed me the same way. Regardless of how many different foods were on the plate, the nurse or aide would feed me one kind of food at a time until that food was completely gone. Take one bite of eggs, eat all of your eggs. Take one bite of hash browns, eat all your hash browns. It was monotonous, and I dreamed of the day I could choose what food went into my mouth.

You can imagine my relief when the doctor said I was finally ready to feed myself. My first "all by myself" meal was breakfast. I was so excited I could hardly place my order. I was going to start with whatever I wanted and move through my plate at my leisure.

I ordered up everything. Ham, bacon, sausage, eggs, toast, pancakes, fruit, yogurt, and best of all, Corn Pops cereal. When the nurse brought me my tray, I had to decide which food would open this masterful meal. Not wanting my cereal to get soggy, I chose Corn Pops.

As giddy as a toddler on Christmas morning, I placed my spoon in the bowl and managed to scoop up one Corn Pop and a little bit of milk. I lifted the spoon to my mouth and realized that just because the doctor said I had the strength in my arms to feed myself didn't mean it was actually a fact. I felt as if I was in an Olympic weightlifting competition as I tried to bring my spoon to my lips. My spoon felt like it weighed a thousand pounds. Before I could take my first bite, my strength gave out, and the Corn Pop dribbled from my spoon.

"If at first you don't succeed, try, try again," I thought as I dipped my spoon into the bowl again. The bite looked just as good as its predecessor, but the results were just as bad. Again and again, I worked to get my first taste of success.

Finally, with every muscle giving complete effort, I got a bite into my mouth. One bite. One Corn Pop with a splash of milk. I relished that Corn Pop. I savored it. I sucked on it until all of its Corn Poppy sweetness had disappeared. Only then did I swallow and bask in the triumph of accomplishing my goal. It was only one Corn Pop, but I had done it myself.

The nurse came to take the tray away and guessed what had happened by the pile of Corn Pops on my hospital gown and the milk spilled from my neck to my stomach. She asked if she could help me with the rest of my breakfast, but I told her I was finished.

I was full, not because of what was in my stomach, but because of how I felt. I had set out that morning to feed myself breakfast, and although it wasn't the biggest breakfast I had ever eaten, I had eaten it by myself. Never before had a Corn Pop tasted so good.

KOLETTE

Quadriplegics have to constantly do "pressure releases." Because they often stay in the same position for long periods of time, they have to make sure that blood flows to the areas of the body that bear the most weight, like the bum and the back.

While sitting in his chair, Jason would lean forward to lift his hind end up for a couple of seconds or hook his arm around the back of his chair and shift himself over. All of these movements would do what the rest of us often do without even thinking—release pressure on the body.

When Jason and I had been married for about twenty years, he developed a calcium deposit on his tailbone. It created increased pressure on that area from the inside out. Because he was always sitting down, his skin began to deteriorate, no matter how many pressure releases he did or how careful we were tending to that area.

Despite our best efforts, the wound got so bad, he required a skin graft. The doctors took a patch of healthy skin from his thigh and placed it over the damaged area. To help the site heal, Jason had to stay in the hospital for three months lying in a special sand bed. The sand bed looked like a large bathtub holding a mattress full of sand. Air moved through the sand and created a low-pressure environment for Jason to rest on while his wound healed.

After three months in the hospital, the first skin graft hadn't healed.
They gave him a three month break, and the surgeon repeated the procedure.
Three months in the hospital on the sand bed, and it failed to work a second time.
Another three month break.
Then they tried one last time, using a specialized vacuum to help the healing process.
It worked.

Jason spent nine out of eighteen months in the hospital.
Coleman and I traveled forty-five minutes each way to visit him
after school.
We celebrated Coleman's fifth and sixth birthdays in that hospital.

Throughout our marriage, Jason and I tried to stay positive, but
when the surgery failed twice and he spent more and more time
away from the life he loved, we both got a little discouraged.

I felt less and less positive. We both started complaining more. I
saw the time I spent with him both in and out of the hospital as
a burden, a hardship that maybe wasn't worth bearing.

I knew I loved Jason, but I was becoming less and less in love
with him.
Little things irritated me.
I noticed ways he didn't measure up.
I tallied up the annoyances.
I didn't feel like he was making an effort to care for me like I
cared for him.

I wanted him to change.
I was bothered that he couldn't see the problem enough to make
a change.
I felt so over it. Over him. Over us.
Jason probably would have been shocked if he'd known that I
didn't really like him all that much anymore.
I didn't tell him, but the feeling sure dominated my thoughts.

Fortunately, I had read enough relationship books and visited
with enough therapists to know that if I wanted to fix how I
was feeling about Jason, I had to fix myself. No one can change
anyone else. And even if I didn't feel like it was my job to be the
one to fix us, wishing that Jason would change wasn't going to
work. As annoying as it was, the change had to come from me.

I didn't like our relationship but that didn't mean that I wanted to be "over us."
Falling in love with Jason in college was a real thing.
Being in love with him for over twenty years was a real thing.
I still wanted that to be my real thing. I just needed to remind myself how to feel it.

I decided to give myself the chance to fall in love with Jason again. I thought that maybe if I remembered the reasons I fell in love in the first place, I could fall in love with him again.

I started writing those reasons down in a notebook.
Honestly, it was a struggle at first. I didn't really want to write them down.
I would sigh and be irritated and think, "Why is this my job?
He should be doing this. He should be treating me the way I deserve to be treated."
And I kept writing.
I reluctantly thought of qualities I loved about him and wrote them down.
I found quotes that described him, printed them out, and glued them to the pages of the book.
I drew little pictures and made doodles of memories we shared.
I added photos of special times together.
I wrote stories of funny moments.

The notebook was one of the best ideas I ever had because of one reason. It helped me remember.

I remembered the times we overcame things, the challenges we fought through, the hard things we accomplished.
I remembered why I admired him. His faith, his perseverance, his humor, his determination, his hope.
I remembered who he had been, who he was, who he was becoming.

I remembered why I fell in love with him in the first place and why we were better together.
I remembered who I was because of him.
I remembered us.

Remembering the good changed me.
The things that irritated me were still there. The annoying behavior was still there.
I just saw it a little differently.
And I actually started liking him again, but it was even better this time.

Seeing the good actually began to fill in the holes of what I thought was missing.

JASON

After breaking my neck, I spent weeks in intensive care. When you're in intensive care, you've got one job, and that's to stay alive. Just take a breath. Then take one more breath after that. That's it. That's all you've got to do. Everything else is taken care of by someone else.

When you get good enough at breathing on your own, they move you to rehab. Rehab is a whole different experience. In rehab, I really started to understand the magnitude of my situation. In rehab, I discovered I couldn't move my hands.

I can't move or feel anything south of the line right under my arms. I can't move or feel anything on the inside of a line drawn down the center of my arm. I can't move my hands at all. In rehab I began to understand all the things I wouldn't be able to do because I couldn't move my hands. It was a very, very long list. Pages and pages long. Discouragingly long.

One night, I made a deal with God. "I will live my life happily every day in a wheelchair, never complaining, if You will just give me my hands. Keep my legs," I pleaded, "just give me back my hands."

At fifteen years old, it seemed like a fair trade, but I knew God wouldn't take the deal unless I worked hard every day. So I did. In therapy I gave everything I had. The work was slow and grueling and tedious, but I knew it would be worth the effort.

Then I met Dan.

Dan's injury was similar to mine. He was confined to a wheelchair, but he had complete use of his arms and hands and a little bit of movement in his legs. In therapy, I sat on the mat, and Dan sat across the room in his chair. The therapist prodded him. "Hey, Dan, let's work on your hands today. Let's strengthen your arms." Dan would shake his head. "All I want to do is look at my legs. Maybe today they'll move. Maybe today they'll work."

I sat across the room feeling incredibly frustrated. This guy had everything I wanted, everything I'd asked God for, but he was so wrapped up in what he didn't have he couldn't see the incredible gift of his hands.

"Don't you see what you have?" I would scream inside my head. "Don't you understand that you have access to blessings and opportunities I can only dream of, and all you talk about is what you don't have?" After a week or so, I couldn't take it anymore. I couldn't watch Dan throw away his chances, chances I wanted so badly. I told my therapist I was done. "Put me in my chair. I'm not doing therapy. I quit."

As I pushed my way back to my room, I noticed a friend's door was open. This friend had the same break in his neck, technically at the same level. I went in to talk with him. I ranted about the raw deal we'd gotten and how unfair it was that we couldn't move our hands.

Rich wore leather braces on his wrists. I had worn similar braces when I had first come to the hospital but no longer needed them. Rich had been in the hospital longer than I had. "Rich," I said, "you don't need those anymore. You've been in the hospital long enough that you can take them off." Rich asked his good, sweet wife, Marilee, to take the brace off one of his wrists. When she took the brace off, his hand went limp. Although we had a similar injury, his neck was broken literally one pinhead higher than mine. Because of that, he couldn't move his wrists at all.

Ashamed, I went back to my room. Was I that much different than Dan? I was so wrapped up in what I didn't have I couldn't see the incredible gift of my wrists. Lying in my bed that night, I looked up at the mirror above my bed. I moved my wrists up and down, up and down, up and down. Each time I lifted my wrists, I thought of one blessing or opportunity that was mine. As I continued to make a list of things I was grateful for, all of that discouragement, all of that despair melted away. I finally understood. There is not enough room in the human heart for both hopelessness and gratitude to exist at the same time.

Occasionally, these feelings of despair and discouragement resurface in my life. Once I'd had an especially frustrating day at school, and I was angry I had to do this wheelchair thing. I pulled out a piece of paper and wrote the numbers one to one hundred. I began to write things I was grateful for. My first twenty-five things were pretty easy: my family, my loyal friends, the elevator in our home. The second twenty-five things were a little harder. The third twenty-five took some serious thinking. By the last twenty-five, I was thankful for lights, drinking glasses, soda. If I could see it in my line of vision, I was grateful for it.

I finished my list, folded it up, and put it in my wallet. Anytime I got down or depressed, I pulled it out and looked at it. Remembering to see the good is my guaranteed way to get back on course.

Because in gratitude, hope shines.

KOLETTE

I've created many gratitude journals in my life.
I have calendars where I write down one thing I'm thankful for each day.
I have photo journals, one photo per day to document my gratitude.
I use daily gratitude apps.
I post lists around my house to remind me what I'm thankful for.
Even that notebook I created for Jason was a kind of gratitude journal.

People asked us all the time how we did it. How we stayed positive in spite of our troubles. For Jason and me, choosing to see the good was always the quickest and most effective way to change our circumstances. Simply because it changed how we felt about our circumstances.

Seeing the good doesn't mean we ignore the hurt.
It doesn't mean we brush our pain and discouragement under the nearest rug.
It doesn't mean we say, "I'm fine," when we feel anything but.

Jason and I never stayed "fine" for long with that approach.
Resentment and bitterness, fear and hopelessness are sure to come running when we gloss over our struggles with a fake declaration that "everything is fine."

Instead, we used our oh-so-tricky two-step "see the good" strategy.
Step 1: Acknowledge the hard thing.
Step 2: Think of something we're grateful for as quickly as possible.

That's the strategy.
The big life-altering stuff, the small daily grind stuff, it seemed to work for all of that.

When Jason and I lived in Connecticut, Jason underwent over twenty surgeries to fix the broken bones and other injuries from his car accident. He was constantly in and out of the hospital.

We lived in a one-bedroom cottage with a loft where I worked.
Our bedroom was small and had two steps going down to it.
Both are what you would call "barriers" for someone in a wheelchair.

We had a little ramp built into the room with a slope that had no hope of passing ADA requirements. Jason would go down the treacherous ramp and make a sharp turn into the bedroom. There was barely enough space for his wheelchair beside the bed.

One particular week, Jason's car was in the shop because an animal had built a nest in the engine. On Sunday morning, instead of taking a well-deserved and completely understandable day off, Jason decided to ride the two miles to church in his wheelchair. I planned to meet him there with the battery charger so he could plug in, charge up, and make it back home when church was over.

The road to the church was winding and hilly.
On the way down the hill, the wheelchair power cut out for a split second.

Jason fell forward on the chair's control knob.
He couldn't sit up to stop his chair, and his hand was stuck on the joystick.
His wheelchair lurched out of control down the hill.
His foot slipped off his footrest and fell.
Then he ran over it.
This pitched him out of his chair and onto the road.

Lying in a heap on the pavement, he called out for help. His quiet quadriplegic yell miraculously reached the ears of a woman watering her plants outside. She came to see what had happened and after being sufficiently startled at what she found, called me. When I got there, I called an ambulance. Jason had broken his shoulder.

A week later, he was in bed in our cottage in the tiny bedroom with the steep ramp.

I was working in my loft when a windstorm whipped around our little cottage. I heard a crack like thunder and looked up right as a tree branch crashed through our roof. I ran down to Jason, and we found ourselves surrounded by thousands of leaves.

A tree had fallen on our cottage.
A really big, one-hundred-foot tall, Connecticut-sized tree.
While Jason was in bed with a broken shoulder.
And our van had been disabled by a little critter's nest.

We found ourselves in a jungle, grateful Jason hadn't been crushed in his bed.

There were tall, beautiful trees all around the cottage property.
Why did this one suddenly come toppling down?

I took a look outside. The tree had grown along the edge of a creek. The roots had grown away from the creek itself, creating only a half-circle root base. That tree was completely uprooted because it had an unstable foundation.

Gratitude is easy and free and instantly accessible, day or night.
It was our foundation.
It was our "You can do this!" plan of attack.
It was our "Never lose hope" protocol.
Because our brains search for evidence that our thoughts are true. As we offer our brains some gratitude, we begin to support and strengthen the good stuff we're telling it to look for.

Windstorms, real or figurative, always blew around us.
They pushed at us and threatened to upend our best efforts to feel joy.
The sooner we deliberately chose to see the good, the better we were at standing our ground.

Gratitude journals and lists are great tools. We use them often. But the resources we go for the most are our thoughts and our words, readily available no matter where we are. No supplies required.

Here's an example:

Situation: "Jason, a tree just fell on our house as you lay in bed with a broken shoulder."
Step 1 - Acknowledge It: "Well, that stinks."
Step 2 – Get to Gratitude:
    "But I'm grateful you didn't get smashed."

Life is hard, but there are good things about it too. In the midst of being covered by branches and leaves, there are still some good things about it.
Gratitude gets us to the good things.

JASON

I broke my neck the summer before my sophomore year of high school. When I returned from the hospital, I began to integrate myself back into the rigors of tenth grade. I started by taking two classes. I went to class in the morning, then my mother picked me up and took me to therapy. When I finished therapy, she returned me to school so that I could go to the final class period of the day.

One day in class, I had a muscle spasm in my leg. Muscle spasms were a common occurrence for me. They made it look like I was moving my leg, but they were a reflex due to my injury. Sometimes my leg would kick out and shake. Sometimes my leg would go up and down, and my foot would tap, tap, tap on my footrest. The muscle spasms happened quite often. I had gotten used to them and thought nothing of it.

This particular day at school, my leg began to tap. My friend Nicole looked at my leg, and her eyes got as big as silver dollars. She jumped out of her chair and yelled, "He's healed!"

I thought, "Who's healed?" The whole class turned around in unison, looked at my leg, and shouted together. "He's healed!" Everyone started jumping up and down, cheering, doing the dance of healing, ordering pizza to celebrate, and preparing for a victory party. Not long into the dance of healing, I realized it was *my* leg they were celebrating.

In the midst of the mayhem, I pulled Nicole to the back of the class and explained that I, in fact, had not been healed. You could almost see the red travel from her neck all the way to her forehead. She went to the front of the class and got everyone's attention. "Uhh, class, I don't know how to tell you this, but he's not healed." The entire class deflated.

Why did Nicole think that right there in class I could be totally and completely healed? It was because she believed. She believed I could be healed. She believed it so much that all she needed was a shred of evidence, the tiniest bit of encouragement, and she was convinced.

Nicole saw the possibilities. Even in the midst of the biggest challenge her friend was facing, she believed that something incredible could happen.

Nicole watched for the good. She waited for it. She anticipated it. Then she saw it.

FACEBOOK POST – NOVEMBER 24, 2019 (DAY 183)

Six months ago today...
I didn't know.

I didn't rush to the hospital.
I did what I always do.
Packed a bag with snacks and things to keep busy.
Gathered a jacket, my Kindle, supplies for a long night in the ER.
I drove my own car.
Got there about 15 minutes after he did.
Because that's what I always did.

I didn't know.

I was calm.
I talked to the doctors.
Trusted that they would figure it out.
I cracked jokes. Laughed.
It's what we always did in hard situations.
It was our strategy to look for the good in every situation.
We always laughed through the hard things.

I chatted with our church leader who was at the hospital with me.
Told him about our goals for the jason&kolette brand.
We talked about podcasts and books and futures and dreams.
At 11:30 p.m. I told him he could go home. Then at 2:14 a.m. Again
at 4:27 a.m. I said we would be fine.
He didn't go.
I kept our parents updated.
It'll be a tough recovery but they're figuring it out, I texted.

I didn't know.

Jason looked at me that last time.
Struggling for oxygen.
They gave him meds to paralyze his whole body and put him to
sleep in order to intubate him. Help him. Save him.

I smiled at him, touched his head, the side of his face, and said,
"It'll be ok."

I thought it would be.
I thought it would be just like every other time.
We have hard things, but we recover.
We keep going.
We do it.

I just did what we always did.
I didn't know that this time would be different.

Sometimes it seems we are surrounded by darkness.
Like there is no hope.
No chance for joy.
No life beyond pain and sorrow and heartache.
Sometimes it's just too hard.
Gratitude is a power.
Gratitude can elbow out the darkness, even if it's just for a moment.

Gratitude is light.
Jason died. It's really hard.
I still feel every day. I still miss him every day.

But Coleman and I know that he is now free of his limitations.
We can't see him, but he is near us. He is helping us.
We know that we will see him again.
We know that we will be together again.
We are missing what is missing now.

But in gratitude, hope shines.
I'm sticking with hope.
And, Jas, I still think it'll be ok.

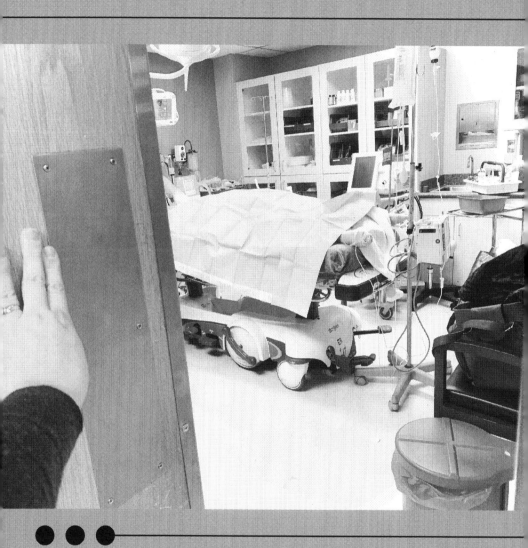

CHAPTER 10
JASON DOES NOT FREEZE TO DEATH

FACEBOOK POST – AUGUST 22, 2019 (DAY 90)

The day got closer.
And closer.
Tuesday, August 20.
Goodbye summer vacation.
Goodbye trips and distractions and playing all day.

First day of school.
First day of lacrosse practice.

School without Dad's before-school father's blessing.
School without Dad inspecting his new school supplies.
School without Dad checking out where his desk was.
School without telling Dad all about the first day.

Lacrosse without Dad driving him to practice.
Lacrosse without Dad calling out, "Coleman J! Let's go!"
Lacrosse without Dad checking the roster, getting his headset mic strapped to his chair, wearing his whistle.
Lacrosse without Dad asking Coleman to grab his Syracuse Youth Lacrosse baseball cap.
Lacrosse without Coach.

Two nights earlier, I had found Coleman in bed, crying a little bit because he missed his dad, holding his necklace with Jason's name stamped into it and reciting the Hall family cheer.

My heart broke.
We cheered the family cheer together.
Then cried a little bit together.
And I told him it's ok to cry.
It's ok to feel sad.
I feel sad too.

And that even though it feels hard, we can do this.
We can do school and lacrosse and everything else.
And it'll get better.

Coleman asked his Grandpa Hall to give him his school blessing.
Because he was the closest thing to having his dad.
We felt Jason with us during that blessing.
Encouraging Coleman. Loving him.

Tuesday, August 20.
We walked into school together.
We went to lacrosse together.

Then I went to the car.
And cried.
Because his coach isn't here.
And his dad isn't here.

Coleman really IS going to crush 5th grade.
First day was awesome.
Old friends, same teacher from last year, he knows the drill.
"How was school?"
"I loved it!" he said.

Lacrosse practice was great.
Some things different but a lot of things the same.
Same fundamentals taught, Dad's assistant coach taking the lead,
same team cheer.
"How was lacrosse?"
"I loved it!" he said.

And I have no doubt that his dad is there for it all. I'm really grateful
I know that.

Tuesday, August 20.
My emotions were right at the surface.
I probably cried a dozen times that day.
But since I like feeling him and remembering him, it was ok. I kinda
like the crying, actually.
Some days I just feel more than others.

Then the next day was better.
Because that's how life is.

First day of school.
First day of lacrosse practice.
Whew. We did it, buddy!

JASON

When I returned home from the hospital after I broke my neck, I tried to find a way to stay involved at my high school as a quadriplegic. My biggest obstacle was sports. Although a 6'2", 300-pound athlete may have looked good on a stats sheet, the 300 pounds included my 200-pound wheelchair—not quite the same asset on the field.

Unable to participate in the sports I loved so much, I started a school spirit club with some of my friends. We called ourselves

"The Rowdies." We had T-shirts printed up, put on pep rallies, and painted our faces at the games. After ballgames, we met at a local pizza place and did all the crazy things high school students do at restaurants after 10:00 p.m. until the place closed or we were "invited" to leave.

One night after driving home from the pizza place, I noticed my parents had parked one car in the garage and the other in the driveway. This was a problem. I was supposed to park my full-sized van in the garage so I could open the automatic doors on my van, roll onto the motorized lift, and lower the lift to the ground. From the garage, there was easy access to our elevator.

Because it was so late and I didn't want to wake my parents, I maneuvered my van as best I could on the driveway. I opened the door to put out the lift, and the icy chill made me shiver. It was a particularly cold late December night. And in Boise, that's saying something.

The lift folded out of my van. I rolled my wheelchair onto the platform and lowered the lift to the ground. The concrete underneath was just a little uneven. With the weight of my wheelchair on the lift, the platform sat flush against the ground, but as my front wheels came off the lift, there was no longer enough weight to keep the lift even on the uneven driveway.

The lift rose just enough to catch the center of my wheelchair. The front wheels were on the ground, but the back wheels weren't touching a thing and my chair only had rear wheel drive. I moved the joystick controller back and forth, but the wheels simply spun in the air. In 1986, I didn't have a smart phone or a flip phone or even a brick phone to call someone for help. I was stuck.

I did everything I could to reach the lift controls behind me, hoping I could move the platform down farther to give my rear wheels a chance at some traction. I couldn't reach the controls.

I thought if I could call out loudly enough for my parents to hear me in the house, they could help me off the lift. I didn't want to wake the whole neighborhood, so I called out softly, "Mom! Dad!"

Nothing. I raised my voice. Still nothing.

I was freezing cold and getting colder by the minute. Not caring who woke up, I yelled at the top of my voice. Still no response from the house. I was convinced that World War III could have started in my front yard and my parents would have slept through it. Giving up on my mom and dad, I yelled the names of our neighbors. "Mr. Nielsen! Mrs. Bishop!"

An hour passed, and I was running out of options. I came up with a brilliant idea. "Fire! Murder!" I screamed. Absolutely no reaction from my neighborhood.

I had one option left. The keys to my van were on a tiny metal rod I held in my hand. If I could throw my keys hard enough, I could break our front window and set off the alarm. Knowing this was my last resort, I took a few practice swings. I aimed carefully, pulled my arm back, and let the keys fly. It was a beautiful throw, perfectly on target. But like a boomerang, the metal rod veered to the left and fell silently on the grass.

Defeated, I tucked my arms into my short-sleeved Rowdies t-shirt and prepared for what I was sure was going to be a long winter's nap.

Suddenly, another thought came to me. "Did you pray?"

"No, I didn't."

"Well, do you think it could hurt?"

I bowed my head. "Heavenly Father, it's really cold. I need help."

Just as I said, "Amen," my mom opened the front door of our house. "Do you need some help?" she asked.

I laughed to myself. *No, Mom, I'm good. Just out here freezing to death.* Not wanting to tempt fate with any smart aleck remarks, I replied in the affirmative.

"I'll get your father."

A neighbor had woken up and heard my faint cries for help. He phoned my parents. My parents realized I wasn't home yet, and Mom came out to check on me. My parents helped me off of the lift and into bed. I was so cold they had to warm me up before I could go to sleep. The temperature had dropped low enough that night that with my poor circulation, I most likely would not have survived.

Something woke our neighbor that night. Something told him to call my parents. I don't believe it was a coincidence, and I don't believe it was luck. Because of a prayer, a great thing—a miraculous thing—saved me that night.

KOLETTE

I used to think that miracles were big things. The things that save a life or change the world.
Those are definitely miracles, no question.
But miracles are so much more than the big things.
Jason's life was saved many times. My life was saved. It was easy to recognize those miracles.
But there were even more miracles in the small moments.
The little actions and decisions that seem insignificant but often lead to a future blessing.

The miracles that change what is possible.

There were miracles when we made a shift in our path, chose a different direction, acted on an impression to move forward in a certain way. Over and over again, listening to each nudge until, by these small miracles, we landed in exactly the right place looking back at each twist and turn saying, "Oh, that's how I ended up here."

Miracles often start long before the adversity comes. Before we realize they are being put into place for some future benefit. Then when we turn our head and look over our shoulder, we see the miracles that dotted the path to get us where we are.

Five years after we married, we were living in Lehi, Utah. Jason worked twenty-five minutes north of our house, selling life insurance and advising clients in financial planning. One day he had an appointment in a town south of Lehi, so he decided to work from home that morning and leave from our house to drive to his appointment at noon.

But he had a feeling he needed to go to the office.
He wondered why.
Was there a person he needed to see or a message he needed to pick up?
He got in his van and drove north to the office, even though it meant he'd have to backtrack south to his appointment later.

Upon arriving at the office, he asked the receptionist if he had any messages.
No.
He asked if any of the other agents needed him.
Nope.
He drove his chair around the hallways so his coworkers could see him, just in case.
Still nothing.

Confused, he got back into his van and headed south.
On the freeway, his left front tire exploded.
He barreled out of control across the Interstate.
That blown tire began his thirteen-month stay in the hospital.

Jason went to the office that day for what seemed like no reason, but because he did, his accident was considered a worker's compensation case. If he had left for his appointment from home rather than the office, he would not have been "at work" when the accident happened.

Our portion of the medical bills exceeded half a million dollars. Jason had to go on disability because he was unable to work. We had excellent health insurance, but it never goes the distance on these things. The fact that Jason qualified for a worker's compensation claim enabled us to pay our obligations, obtain the correct care for Jason, and maintain our young-married-couple simple standard of living.

When Jason went into the office that day he was not thinking about our future. He just received an impression to go and acted on the thought. He listened.

The decision to go into the office didn't take away the accident.
It didn't take away the thirteen months spent in the hospital.
It didn't take away the suffering of others also involved in the crash.
It didn't take away ten years of recovery and over thirty surgeries.
It didn't take away the constant pain.
It didn't take away what felt like an endless struggle.
It didn't take away the overwhelming discouragement.

But that decision made it a little easier. Easier for us to navigate the devastating financial burden of the accident.
That impression to go into the office first was a miracle. That decision to listen was a miracle.

Miracles often go before us. They prepare the path for when we face challenges. We may not recognize them for what they are at the time, but miracles often stand by our side, ready to become the reason we can overcome.

The burden is maybe a little less heavy.

The pain is possibly a little more bearable.

The heartache is eased just a bit.

All of those things feel like miracles to me.

It took over ten years for Jason to recover from that car accident. About seven years into the recovery, we returned to Utah after living in Connecticut where Jason's parents had helped us with Jason's rehabilitation. The miracle of Worker's Compensation payments was a gift, but it wasn't quite enough to help us cover all of our medical expenses. We had $50,000 in medical debt.

Needless to say, our apartment in Draper, Utah was a hodgepodge of hand-me-downs and mismatched furniture. Piles of bricks held up the television shelf in our bedroom, and our sofa was covered in quilts to hide the worn spots. The bathroom wasn't set up for Jason's needs, but we made do with that we had.

My brother and I had started our scrapbook company the year before, and we were trying to grow our business on a shoestring budget. The extra bedroom in our apartment was company headquarters, and we kept the product inventory in a storage unit.

Money was tight.

Jason's pain was chronic and intense.

His energy level low.

His medical aide got him into his wheelchair at noon each day and helped him lay down again at about 4:00 each afternoon. The amount of medication required to manage his pain made him unable to function.

Jason was too sick to pursue fertility treatments, and we didn't have the money even if he had been healthy.

Jason was unable to work and unable to help me make decisions for our family.

I was on my own.

I wondered if I would ever be able to get us out of debt.

I wondered if we would ever have a home that was accessible for Jason.

I wondered if we would ever be able to have a child.

I wondered if I would ever get my husband back.

While reading the Bible one day, I came across a story in the book of Joshua. God told Joshua to lead the Israelites into Canaan. They had been waiting forty years to enter the promised land, and the time had come. But they had a problem. They needed to cross the mighty River Jordan, but there was no way to do so with so many people. They needed a miracle.

"And Joshua said unto the people, Sanctify yourselves: for tomorrow the Lord will do wonders among you." Joshua 3:5

Joshua told the people to sanctify themselves, or to make themselves holy.

The next morning, the priests carried the Ark of the Covenant before the people.

They traveled to the edge of the water.

The priests stepped into the flowing river with the ark.

The waters stood up in a heap as if they'd been stopped by a wall.

The Israelites walked across dry land into the promised land.

I read this story and wondered about wonders.

I wondered about the sacrifices Joshua asked the Israelites to make.

I wondered about the promises he gave them if they obeyed.

And I wondered if that same principle would work for us.

In that little apartment, we were standing at the edge of our own River Jordan.

I saw no way to cross to the opposite bank of our struggles.
The river was too big.

We needed wonders.
We needed miracles.

I decided to find out for myself if Joshua 3:5 was true.
I went to the temple, a place where members of our church can go to serve those who have gone before us, gain spiritual instruction, and feel peace.
I prayed while I was there.
Is this scripture true?
Can I sanctify myself too?
Can the Lord do wonders for me too?

My mind and heart filled with the love of God and Jesus Christ.
It surrounded me and strengthened me.
I felt answers to my questions.
Yes, I can sanctify myself. I can become more holy.
Yes, I can receive wonders.

I decided to try it for myself.

Since "sanctify yourself" means to become "more holy," I thought that attending the temple was a good place for me to start.

I resolved to go to the temple once a week for six weeks.
And I prayed that I might know other ways that I could sanctify myself. Realistic ways.
I was the caregiver for Jason, the breadwinner for our family, and the owner of a new company. How could I actually sanctify myself when every nook and cranny of my life was already filled with stress, obligations, and hard work?
I prayed to know what sanctification looked like for me.

I went to the temple every week for six weeks.

I began to have other thoughts, other impressions about things I could do.
I tried to listen carefully to these whisperings from God.

I decided to study my scriptures every day for a few minutes.
I read inspiring talks and articles from church leaders each week.
On the days I went to the temple, I listened to uplifting music, as I ran errands or worked. I tried to keep the peace of the temple with me all day.

I wrote down my spiritual experiences in a journal.
I had a feeling that wonders were going to come, and I wanted to remember them. My "Chronicles of the Road to Wonders" began as a simple Word document on my computer and became pages filled with spiritual thoughts, feelings, experiences, and miracles over the next two years.

After the first six weeks of temple visits, I decided to continue my weekly temple goal for three months.
When three months passed, I decided I could do it until the end of the year, which would be approximately eight months.
Once the end of year came, I thought, "I might as well go a full year."
Then another year.
I went to the temple each week for two years, listening to my music on temple days and writing in my spiritual journal.

The wonders started to happen.

My income from Colorbök royalties and teaching opportunities paid off our medical debt.
That was a miracle.

I received a licensing deal with Hampton Art, a stamping company. Using my artwork, they became the first to offer one-

dollar stamps sold through a major crafting retail chain.
That was a miracle.

My brother and I worked our guts out to build our company without incurring debt. After two years, we put our little scrapbook company up for sale so that I could pursue licensed design work fulltime. We set a sell-by date of February 28. If our company hadn't sold by then, we would simply close our doors. Our company sold on February 27 and banked the money.
That was a miracle.

I had a goal to save $100,000 for a down payment on a handicap-accessible home.
We spent money only on necessities and saved everything else. We moved into that home twenty-three months after I read Joshua 3:5.
That was a miracle.

Jason started working with a new pain specialist.
She implanted a pain pump, which delivered miniscule amounts of medication directly to his spinal column.
The medication delivery system cleared his mind. His eyes sparkled again. He had more energy. He could stay up longer each day.
Jason became a new person.
I had my husband back. He had himself back.
That was a miracle.

We set a goal to try in vitro fertilization.
It failed the first time.
It worked the second time.
That was a miracle.

We still had hard things.
There were hospital stays, pain, and struggle.
But we saw wonders too.

JASON

When I ran down that sand dune and dove into the water at Lake Powell thirty-three years ago, I lost the use of my body in a split second. I almost drowned because I was helpless in the water, unable to lift my head above the surface for air.

God gave me a miracle that day. Somehow, I was able to rise up out of the water and stretch my arm into the air. For you, that might not be a miracle, but for me, even after years of physical therapy, I still cannot raise my arm above my head. My family saw the terror on my face and pulled me out of the water. I had received my first lifesaving miracle. But it certainly wasn't my last.

I believe in miracles.

KOLETTE

Thirty-three years after that fateful day at Lake Powell, I was sitting right next to Jason, folding our laundry, when he began struggling for breath.
I called the ambulance.
I was in the emergency room when they decided to intubate him.
I saw him look up at me with panic in his eyes, unable to speak because his mouth and nose were covered by an oxygen mask.
I put my hand on the side of his face, smiled, and told him it was going to be ok.
And I believed it.

I was there when they tried to suction fluid from his lung cavity.
I was there when it didn't work.
I was there when the nurse stayed glued to his side so she could keep him breathing.
I was there when the team did compressions on his chest to get his heart going again.
I was there when his heart stopped beating for the last time.

But I was also there for twenty-seven years.
I was there when he lived through the night after the doctor said he wouldn't.
I was there when the dangerous fluid in his body drained out at a record pace.
I was there when the doctor inserted a pump to manage Jason's pain.

I was there when a forward-thinking surgeon performed three surgeries on Jason's hand at the same time, giving him the ability to grip his thumb and finger together by simply lifting his wrist.
I was there when they reconstructed his knee to bend properly in his wheelchair.
I was there when they grafted bone and skin to allow him to sit up properly.
I was there for every hospital stay, whether it was one night or three months.
I was there when an infection went septic, I was there when it happened again ten years later.
I was there when in vitro worked.

I was there when Jason lived. Time and time again, in spite of what should have happened, he lived. We became parents. He was the lacrosse coach. He was a motivational speaker. He kept rolling, stronger than ever during his last few years. Healthier than ever.
I was there for the miracles.

And I was there when Jason died.
I was shocked and saddened and stunned.
I still feel a gaping hole left by the man who kept fighting.
I still long for our story to end differently.
I still see him around the corner of every thought in my mind.
But I also know that Jason would be here if he was supposed to be here.
Because for twenty-seven years, I've seen him come back from

the brink of death again and again.
I've seen the miracles that kept him here.

Now I am grieving.
I'm missing my partner, my best friend, my love.
I'm missing the person I told things to.
I'm missing the person who loved me for almost three decades.

I feel sad for the people who didn't get the chance to meet Jason Hall. He took the time to know people. He was funny. He taught you things. You were a better person if you knew Jason.

Some moments are so raw they take my breath away. I find myself going about my day, forgetting he's gone. "I can't wait to tell Jason that funny thing when he gets home," or "Jason will know how to connect that cord. I'll ask him when he gets here." Then comes the inevitable punch in the gut when I remember that he won't be coming home. I'm surprised over and over again that he really isn't here anymore.

"He's away for a while," I often think.
"No wait," I remember, "he's away forever."
And I grieve.

Life without Jason is hard. The twenty-seven years with him shaped who I am. Who we both are.
We are hopeful. We overcome. We are resilient. We are optimistic. We work hard. We serve others. We live with faith. We love. We are the Halls.

We weren't perfect.
We made mistakes.
We almost gave up. Lots of times.
We often felt overwhelmed, discouraged, and angry.
We wished that the hard things weren't necessary.

But we still tried.
We kept the faith, we kept the hope, and we kept trying.

I know what miracles look like.
I know they are not just things we talk about but never witness.
I have seen solutions appear where there weren't any before.
I have seen people who are there at the right moment to lend a hand.
I have felt the comfort of God's love encircle me, strengthen me.
I have prayed for help and listened for answers.
I have felt healing.
I have felt peace.
I have felt hope.
I have experienced miracles.

Jason is gone.
This is hard.
But I will do what we've always done.
And the miracles will continue.
That much I know for sure.

FACEBOOK POST - SEPTEMBER 13, 2019 (DAY 112)

Jason has FOMO.
Fear of Missing Out.
I say "has" because I'm 99.9% sure that he still has it up in heaven.
Coleman has it too.

Just like his ability to make friends and his confidence speaking in public, Coleman got FOMO from his dad.

They love to be part of the action.
They wrestle with what to do when they have to make a choice between two awesome things.
They truly regret missing out.

About half an hour after Jason died, Coleman woke up and called me at the hospital. I had left him at home at 10:00 pm with our aide as his babysitter. Coleman had already gone to bed, and I had fully expected to be home by the time he woke up that morning. Things didn't go as planned.

"Mom, where are you?"
"We're at the hospital. Dad got sick last night. Grandma is going to bring you here." And trying to sound like this was going to be just a normal day, I added, "Get your backpack ready for school and bring it with you."

This wasn't my typical "Dad's in the Hospital" behavior. Usually I came home, drove the carpool to school, and then we would visit dad together after school.

He knew that.
"Mom, where are you?" he asked again.
"We're at the hospital. It's ok. I'll see you soon."

Just after 7:00 am I met him in the ICU hallway, wrapped him in my arms, and said, "Coleman, Dad got sick last night, and he died."

I knelt on the tile floor as his head went to my shoulder and we wept together.

I took him in to see his dad.
The warrior who fought to the bitter end.
The man who loved being a dad more than anything else.

We sat in a chair together right by his bed.
I whispered how Jason's heart beat for his son during those last minutes.
I whispered that now he could run and play lacrosse and could do everything he couldn't do in a wheelchair.

I whispered that he loves us so much.
Tucked into my lap, Coleman whispered back, "Mom, what are we going to do?"

"It's going to be really hard, but we can do this."

Sitting together with Jason was a special time. A sacred time of feeling close to Jason and close to each other.

Other friends and family rushed to the hospital to offer support. Coleman and I stuck together. When he was ready to leave the hospital room, we took a walk down the hall. Then went back to Jason's room again after a while to sit by his side once more.

At 8:10 a.m. we were sitting in a special area reserved for family. I knew Coleman had an end-of-the-year party at school that day.

I asked him what he wanted to do about school.
He said, "I don't really want to go...but it's Bend the Rules Day."
There it was. FOMO.
I had to smile when he said that. Of course he wouldn't want to miss Bend the Rules Day! Who would??? It was our school PTA fundraiser...we paid money so he could break the rules for one day!

His Hubba Bubba Bubble Tape was making a circular bulge in his front pocket.
He had his special pen in his backpack because he didn't have to use a pencil that day.
He was ready to do the whole list of scheduled rule-breaking activities.

But I also knew that we needed to be together that day. There was no way I could just drop him off at school by himself and spend the day without him.
I asked him, "What if I go to school with you?"
"That's a good idea," he said.

So the day Jason died, I went to fourth grade.
We told the principal together.
We told his teacher together.
We sat at the table on the side of the room while the principal told the class.
"Coleman's dad died this morning."
All thirty-one of us were sad together.

For the next six hours we sat at that table while Coleman took his spelling test, did his math, chewed his Hubba Bubba.
He received hugs and kind words from his classmates.
They dropped off notes and drawings and little gifts from their desks.

He went to the rule-breaking dance party in the library.
He played football at recess.

When they announced over the intercom that it was time for the fourth graders to break the ultimate rule of all and RUN in the halls, I said, "I bet Dad wants to run with you."
He grinned and took off to the designated meeting place.
Coleman came back breathing a little heavier. "Mom! I think I beat Dad!"

We got a lot of love that day.
A lot of compassion and care and support from our school community.
It ended up being the perfect place to be on the worst day of our lives.

Yes, his dad died that day, but at least Coleman didn't have to miss Bend the Rules Day too.

ABOUT THE AUTHORS •••—

Kolette Hall is a mother, a writer, and a recent widow. She has a master's degree in education, has created thousands of scrapbooking products as a licensed designer in the crafting world, and is a certified life coach. Kolette's superpower is planning with a purpose, and she organizes her closets for fun. Her favorite role is that of mother to her son, Coleman, who is quite possibly the most awesome kid alive. Kolette and Coleman live in northern Utah.

Jason Hall

was a father, financial planner, and quadriplegic. Jason broke his neck when he was fifteen years old and lived the rest of his life in a wheelchair. He was a popular motivational speaker, inspiring thousands of people with his stories of optimism, perseverance, and grit. He cheered for the Dallas Cowboys his whole life and might have been the most loyal, strong and true BYU fan in the stadium. Jason passed away unexpectedly in 2019. He and Kolette were married for twenty-seven years.

THANK
YOU ● ● ● ──────

Jason talked of writing a book for twenty-seven years. He started and stopped, started and stopped, because his body just couldn't keep up with his dream.
Then we got serious. Hired Craig Case and Jennifer Beckstrand to help make it happen.
A few months later, Jason died.
The book stopped again.
I waited. Jason waited.

And then things started rolling.

Thank you, Craig and Jennifer, for being there at the beginning, always believing in this project. Believing in Jason. Believing in us. Jennifer, your expertise and patience astound me. Thank you for walking this path through grief with me.

Thank you to our readers, who offered thoughtful edits and tremendous encouragement that we were on the right track. Kristen Dayley, your loving and meticulous review became our key reference for publishing.

Courtney Hackman, little did we know that your mentorship on how to write a Facebook ad would lead me to find my voice as a writer. I learned a new talent at age forty-eight because of you! Christina Marcano, your beautiful work formatting this project and getting it ready to print is so much better than I imagined. McKenna Bullock, thank you for seeing what was possible long before it actually happened and for being 100% ready to propel this project out into the world.

I have been driven to move this project forward because of the continuous support from people in every corner of our lives. You have cheered us on. You have asked for more. You have offered pure love. This book is full of stories of you! Thank you, friends.

To our family. You have watched and experienced all of the struggles found here in this book. And many more. You have been there for the despair and for the overcoming. You have been a part of the learning, the laughter, and the miracles.
Jason is still the most loyal person I know – and his loyalty first is to his family.
That has not changed. He loves you. I love you.
You are happily and irrevocably woven into every moment of our journey.
Jason is with us. With you. Next to you.
Still loyal. Still strong. Still true.

Made in the USA
Las Vegas, NV
07 December 2021

36313126R10125